THE ROAD
TO SERFDOM

by

F. A. HAYEK

ROUTLEDGE

First published 1944
Published as a Routledge Paperback 1962
Reissued 1971
by Routledge & Kegan Paul Ltd.
ARK edition published by Routledge & Kegan Paul plc 1986

Reprinted in paperback by Routledge 1991, 1993
11 New Fetter Lane, London EC4P 4EE

Printed and bound in Great Britain by
Mackays of Chatham PLC, Chatham, Kent

ISBN 0–415–06560–7

TO
THE SOCIALISTS
OF
ALL PARTIES

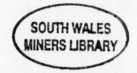

PREFACE

WHEN a professional student of social affairs writes a political book, his first duty is plainly to say so. This is a political book. I do not wish to disguise this by describing it, as I might perhaps have done, by the more elegant and ambitious name of an essay in social philosophy. But, whatever the name, the essential point remains that all I shall have to say is derived from certain ultimate values. I hope I have adequately discharged in the book itself a second and no less important duty : to make it clear beyond doubt what these ultimate values are on which the whole argument depends.

There is, however, one thing I want to add to this. Though this is a political book, I am as certain as anyone can be that the beliefs set out in it are not determined by my personal interests. I can discover no reason why the kind of society which seems to me desirable should offer greater advantages to me than to the great majority of the people of this country. In fact, I am always told by my socialist colleagues that as an economist I should occupy a much more important position in the kind of society to which I am opposed—provided, of course, that I could bring myself to accept their views. I feel equally certain that my opposition to these views is not due to their being different from those with which I have grown up, since they are the very views which I held as a young man and which have led me to make the study of economics my profession. For those who, in the current fashion, seek interested motives in every profession of a political opinion, I may, perhaps, be allowed to add that I have every possible reason for *not* writing or publishing this book. It is certain to offend many people with whom I wish to live on friendly terms ; it has forced me to put aside work for which I feel better qualified and to which I attach greater importance in the long run ; and, above all, it is certain to prejudice the reception of the results of the more strictly academic work to which all my inclinations lead me.

If in spite of this I have come to regard the writing of this book as a duty which I must not evade, this was mainly due to a peculiar and serious feature of the discussions of problems of future economic policy at the present time, of which the public is scarcely sufficiently aware. This is the fact that the majority of economists have now for some years been absorbed by the war machine, and silenced by their official positions, and that in consequence public opinion on these problems is to an alarming extent guided by amateurs and cranks, by people who have an axe to grind or a pet panacea to sell. In these circumstances one who still has the leisure for literary work is hardly entitled to keep to himself apprehensions which current tendencies must create in the minds of many who cannot publicly express them—though in different circumstances I should have gladly left the discussion of questions of national policy to those who are both better authorised and better qualified for the task.

The central argument of this book was first sketched in an article entitled " Freedom and the Economic System," which appeared in the *Contemporary Review* for April, 1938, and was later reprinted in an enlarged form as one of the " Public Policy Pamphlets ", edited by Professor H. D. Gideonse for the University of Chicago Press (1939). I have to thank the editors and publishers of both these publications for permission to reproduce certain passages from them.

London School of Economics,

Cambridge, December, 1943

CONTENTS

INTRODUCTION

Few discoveries are more irritating than those which expose
the pedigree of ideas.

Lord Acton.

CONTEMPORARY events differ from history in that we do
not know the results they will produce. Looking back, we
can assess the significance of past occurrences and trace the
consequences they have brought in their train. But while history
runs its course, it is not history to us. It leads us into an unknown
land and but rarely can we get a glimpse of what lies ahead. It
would be different if it were given to us to live a second time
through the same events with all the knowledge of what we have
seen before. How different would things appear to us, how
important and often alarming would changes seem that we now
scarcely notice ! It is probably fortunate that man can never
have this experience and knows of no laws which history must
obey.

Yet, although history never quite repeats itself, and just because
no development is inevitable, we can in a measure learn from the
past to avoid a repetition of the same process. One need not
be a prophet to be aware of impending dangers. An accidental
combination of experience and interest will often reveal events
to one man under aspects which few yet see.

The following pages are the product of an experience as near
as possible to twice living through the same period—or at
least twice watching a very similar evolution of ideas. While
this is an experience one is not likely to gain in one country, it
may in certain circumstances be acquired by living in turn for
long periods in different countries. Though the influences to
which the trend of thought is subject in most civilised nations
are to a large extent similar, they do not necessarily operate at
the same time or at the same speed. Thus, by moving from one
country to another, one may sometimes twice watch similar
phases of intellectual development. The senses have then become
peculiarly acute. When one hears for a second time opinions
expressed or measures advocated which one has first met twenty
or twenty-five years ago, they assume a new meaning as symptoms
of a definite trend. They suggest, if not the necessity, at least
the probability, that developments will take a similar course.

It is necessary now to state the unpalatable truth that it is
Germany whose fate we are in some danger of repeating. The
danger is not immediate, it is true, and conditions in this country
are still so remote from those witnessed in recent years in Germany

as to make it difficult to believe that we are moving in the same direction. Yet, though the road be long, it is one on which it becomes more difficult to turn back as one advances. If in the long run we are the makers of our own fate, in the short run we are the captives of the ideas we have created. Only if we recognise the danger in time can we hope to avert it.

It is not to the Germany of Hitler, the Germany of the present war, that this country bears yet any resemblance. But students of the currents of ideas can hardly fail to see that there is more than a superficial similarity between the trend of thought in Germany during and after the last war and the present current of ideas in this country. There exists now in this country certainly the same determination that the organisation of the nation we have achieved for purposes of defence shall be retained for the purposes of creation. There is the same contempt for nineteenth-century liberalism, the same spurious " realism " and even cynicism, the same fatalistic acceptance of " inevitable trends ". And at least nine out of every ten of the lessons which our most vociferous reformers are so anxious we should learn from this war are precisely the lessons which the Germans did learn from the last war and which have done much to produce the Nazi system. We shall have opportunity in the course of this book to show that there are a large number of other points where, at an interval of fifteen to twenty-five years, we seem to follow the example of Germany. Although one does not like to be reminded, it is not so many years since the socialist policy of that country was generally held up by progressives as an example to be imitated, just as in more recent years Sweden has been the model country to which progressive eyes were directed. All those whose memory goes further back know how deeply, for at least a generation before the last war, German thought and German practice influenced ideals and policy in this country.

The author has spent about half of his adult life in his native Austria, in close touch with German intellectual life, and the other half in the United States and England. In the dozen years in which this country has now become his home he has become increasingly convinced that at least some of the forces which have destroyed freedom in Germany are also at work here, and that the character and the source of this danger are, if possible, even less understood than they were in Germany. The supreme tragedy is still not seen that in Germany it was largely people of goodwill, men who were admired and held up as models in this country, who prepared the way, if they did not actually create, the forces which now stand for everything they detest. Yet our chance of averting a similar fate depends on our facing the danger and on our being prepared to revise even our most cherished hopes and ambitions if they should prove to be the source of the danger. There are few signs yet that we have the intellectual courage to admit to ourselves that we may have been wrong. Few are ready to recognise that the rise of Fascism and Nazism was not a reaction against the socialist trends of the preceding period, but a necessary outcome of those tendencies. This is a truth which most people were unwilling to see even when the similarities of many of the repellent features of the internal regimes in communist Russia and national-socialist Germany were widely recognised. As a result, many who think themselves infinitely superior to the aberrations of Nazism and sincerely hate all its manifestations, work at the same time for ideals whose realisation would lead straight to the abhorred tyranny.

All parallels between developments in different countries are, of course, deceptive ; but I am not basing my argument mainly on such parallels. Nor am I arguing that these developments are inevitable. If they were, there would be no point in writing this. They can be prevented if people realise in time where their efforts may lead. But till recently there was little hope that any attempt to make them see the danger would be successful. It seems, however, as if the time were now ripe for a fuller discussion of the whole issue. Not only is the problem now more widely recognised, there are also special reasons which at this juncture make it imperative that we should face the issues squarely.

It will, perhaps, be said that this is not the time to raise an issue on which opinions clash sharply. But the socialism of which we speak is not a party matter, and the questions which we are discussing have little to do with the questions at dispute between political parties. It does not affect our problem that some groups may want less socialism than others, that some want socialism mainly in the interest of one group and others in that of another. The important point is that, if we take the people whose views influence developments, they are now in this country in some measure all socialists. If it is no longer fashionable to emphasise that " we are all socialists now ", this is so merely because the fact is too obvious. Scarcely anybody doubts that we must continue to move towards socialism, and most people are merely trying to deflect this movement in the interest of a particular class or group.

It is because nearly everybody wants it that we are moving in this direction. There are no objective facts which make it inevitable. We shall have to say something about the alleged inevitability of " planning " later. The main question is where this movement will lead us. Is it not possible that if the people whose convictions now give it an irresistible momentum began to see what only a few yet apprehend, they would recoil in horror and abandon the quest which for half a century has engaged so many people of goodwill ? Where these common beliefs of our generation will lead us is a problem not for one party but for every one of us, a problem of the most momentous significance. Is there a greater tragedy imaginable than that in our endeavour consciously to shape our future in accordance with high ideals, we should in fact unwittingly produce the very opposite of what we have been striving for ?

There is an even more pressing reason why at this time we should seriously endeavour to understand the forces which have created National Socialism : that this will enable us to understand our enemy and the issue at stake between us. It cannot be denied that there is yet little recognition of the positive ideals for which we are fighting. We know that we are fighting for freedom to shape our life according to our own ideas. That is a great deal, but not enough. It is not enough to give us the firm beliefs which we need to resist an enemy who uses propaganda as one of his main weapons not only in the most blatant but also in the most subtle forms. It is still more insufficient when we have to counter this propaganda among the people in the countries under his control and elsewhere, where the effect of this propaganda will not disappear with the defeat of the Axis powers. It is not enough if we are to show to others that what we are fighting for is worth their support, and not enough to guide us in the building of a new Europe safe against the dangers to which the old one has succumbed.

It is a lamentable fact that the English in their dealings with the dictators before the war, not less than in their attempts at propaganda and in the discussion of their war aims, have shown an inner insecurity and uncertainty of aim which can be explained only by confusion about their own ideals and the nature of the differences which separated them from the enemy. We have been misled as much because we have refused to believe that the enemy was sincere in the profession of some beliefs which we shared as because we believed in the sincerity of some of his other claims. Have not the parties of the Left as well as those of the Right been deceived by believing that the National-Socialist Party was in the service of the capitalists and opposed to all forms of socialism ? How many features of Hitler's system have not been recommended to us for imitation from the most unexpected quarters, unaware that they are an integral part of that system and incompatible with the free society we hope to preserve ? The number of dangerous mistakes we have made before and since the outbreak of war because we do not understand the opponent with whom we are faced is appalling. It seems almost as if we did not want to understand the development which has produced totalitarianism because such an understanding might destroy some of the dearest illusions to which we are determined to cling.

We shall never be successful in our dealings with the Germans till we understand the character and the growth of the ideas which now govern them. The theory which is once again put forth, that the Germans as such are inherently vicious, is hardly tenable and not very creditable to those who hold it. It dishonours the long series of Englishmen who during the past hundred years have gladly taken over what was best, and not only what was best, in German thought. It overlooks the fact that when eighty years ago John Stuart Mill was writing his great essay *On Liberty* he drew his inspiration, more than from any other men, from two Germans, Goethe and Wilhelm von Humboldt,[1] and forgets the fact that two of the most influential intellectual forebears of National Socialism, Thomas Carlyle and Houston Stewart Chamberlain, were a Scot and an Englishman. In its cruder forms this view is a disgrace to those who by maintaining it adopt the worst features of German racial theories. The problem is not why the Germans as such are vicious, which congenitally they are probably no more than other peoples, but to determine the circumstances which during the last seventy years have made possible the progressive growth and the ultimate victory of a particular set of ideas, and why in the end this victory has brought the most vicious elements among them to the top. Mere hatred of everything German, instead of the particular ideas which now dominate the Germans is, moreover, very dangerous, because it blinds those who indulge in it against a real threat. It is to be feared that this attitude is frequently merely a kind of escapism, caused by an unwillingness to recognise tendencies which are not confined to Germany, and by reluctance to reexamine, and if necessary to discard, beliefs which we have taken over from the Germans and by which we are still as much deluded as the Germans were. It is doubly dangerous because the contention that only the peculiar wickedness of the Germans has produced the Nazi system is likely to become the excuse for forcing on us the very institutions which have produced that wickedness.

The interpretation of the developments in Germany and Italy about to be proffered in this book is very different from that given by most foreign observers and by the majority of exiles from those countries. But if this interpretation is correct, it will also

---

[1] As some people may think this statement exaggerated, the testimony of Lord Morley may be worth quoting, who in his *Recollections* speaks of the " acknowledged point " that the main argument of the essay *On Liberty* " was not original but came from Germany ".

explain why it is almost impossible for a person who, like most of the exiles and the foreign correspondents of English and American newspapers, holds the now prevalent socialist views, to see those events in the proper perspective.[1] The superficial and misleading view, which sees in National-Socialism merely a reaction fomented by those whose privileges or interests were threatened by the advance of socialism, was naturally supported by all those who, although they were at one time active in the movement of ideas that has led to National-Socialism, have stopped at some point of that development and, by the conflict into which this brought them with the Nazis, were forced to leave their country. But the fact that they were numerically the only significant opposition to the Nazis means no more than that in the wider sense practically all Germans had become socialists, and that liberalism in the old sense had been driven out by socialism. As we hope to show, the conflict in existence between the National-Socialist " Right " and the " Left " in Germany is the kind of conflict that will always arise between rival socialist factions. If this interpretation is correct it means, however, that many of those socialist refugees, in clinging to their beliefs, are now, though with the best will in the world, helping to lead their adopted country the way which Germany has gone.

I know that many of my English friends have sometimes been shocked by the semi-Fascist views they would occasionally hear expressed by German refugees, whose genuinely socialist convictions could not be doubted. But while these English observers put this down to their being Germans, the true explanation is that they were socialists whose experience had carried them several stages beyond that yet reached by socialists in this country. It is true, of course, that German socialists have found much support in their country from certain features of the Prussian tradition ; and this kinship between Prussianism and socialism, in which in Germany both sides gloried, gives additional support to our main contention.[2] But it would be a mistake to believe

[1] How thoroughly the views held in all quarters, even the most conservative, of a whole country can be coloured by the predominant Left bias of the foreign correspondents of its Press, is well illustrated by the views almost universally held in America about the relations between Great Britain and India. The Englishman who wishes to see events on the European Continent in the proper perspective must seriously consider the possibility that his views may have been distorted in precisely the same manner, and for the same reasons. This is in no way meant to reflect on the sincerity of the views of American and English foreign correspondents. But anyone who knows the kind of native circles with which foreign correspondents are likely to have close contacts, will have no difficulty in understanding the sources of this bias.

[2] That there did exist a certain kinship between socialism and the organisation of the Prussian State, consciously organised from the top as in no other country, is undeniable and was freely recognised already by the early French socialists.

that the specific German rather than the socialist element produced totalitarianism. It was the prevalence of socialist views and not Prussianism that Germany had in common with Italy and Russia—and it was from the masses and not from the classes steeped in the Prussian tradition, and favoured by it, that National-Socialism arose.

Long before the ideal of running the whole state on the same principles as a single factory was to inspire nineteenth-century socialism, the Prussian poet Novalis had already deplored that " no other state has ever been administered so much like a factory as Prussia since the death of Frederick William." (Cf. Novalis [Friedrich von Hardenberg], *Glauben und Liebe, oder der König und die Königin,* 1798.)

CHAPTER I

THE ABANDONED ROAD

A programme whose basic thesis is, not that the system of
free enterprise for profit has failed in this generation, but that
it has not yet been tried.

F. D. Roosevelt.

WHEN the course of civilisation takes an unexpected turn,
when instead of the continuous progress which we have come to
expect, we find ourselves threatened by evils associated by us
with past ages of barbarism, we blame naturally anything but
ourselves. Have we not all striven according to our best lights,
and have not many of our finest minds incessantly worked to
make this a better world ? Have not all our efforts and hopes
been directed towards greater freedom, justice, and prosperity ?
If the outcome is so different from our aims, if, instead of freedom
and prosperity, bondage and misery stare us in the face, is it not
clear that sinister forces must have foiled our intentions, that we
are the victims of some evil power which must be conquered
before we can resume the road to better things ? However much
we may differ when we name the culprit, whether it is the wicked
capitalist or the vicious spirit of a particular nation, the stupidity
of our elders, or a social system not yet, although we have struggled
against it for half a century, fully overthrown—we all are, or
at least were until recently, certain of one thing : that the
leading ideas which during the last generation have become
common to most people of goodwill and have determined the
major changes in our social life cannot have been wrong. We
are ready to accept almost any explanation of the present crisis
of our civilisation except one : that the present state of the
world may be the result of genuine error on our own part, and
that the pursuit of some of our most cherished ideals have
apparently produced results utterly different from those which
we expected.

While all our energies are directed to bringing this war to a
victorious conclusion, it is sometimes difficult to remember that
even before the war the values for which we are now fighting
were threatened here and destroyed elsewhere. Though for the
time being the different ideals are represented by hostile nations
fighting for their existence, we must not forget that this conflict
has grown out of a struggle of ideas within what, not so long ago,
was a common European civilisation ; and that the tendencies
which have culminated in the creation of the totalitarian systems

8

were not confined to the countries which have succumbed to them. Though the first task must now be to win the war, to win it will only gain us another opportunity to face the basic problems and to find a way of averting the fate which has overtaken kindred civilisations.

Now, it is somewhat difficult to think of Germany and Italy, or of Russia, not as different worlds, but as products of a development of thought in which we have shared ; it is, at least so far as our enemies are concerned, easier and more comforting to think that they are entirely different from us and that what happened there cannot happen here. Yet the history of these countries in the years before the rise of the totalitarian system showed few features with which we are not familiar. The external conflict is a result of a transformation of European thought in which others have moved so much faster as to bring them into irreconcilable conflict with our ideals, but which has not left us unaffected.

That a change of ideas, and the force of human will, have made the world what it is now, though men did not foresee the results, and that no spontaneous change in the facts obliged us thus to adapt our thought, is perhaps particularly difficult for the English to see, just because in this development the English have, fortunately for them, lagged behind most of the European peoples. We still think of the ideals which guide us and have guided us for the past generation, as ideals only to be realised in the future, and are not aware how far in the last twenty-five years they have already transformed, not only the world, but also this country. We still believe that until quite recently we were governed by what are vaguely called nineteenth-century ideas or the principle of *laissez-faire*. Compared with some other countries, and from the point of view of those impatient to speed up the change, there may be some justification for such belief. But although till 1931 this country had followed only slowly on the path on which others had led, even by then we had moved so far that only those whose memory goes back to the years before the last war know what a liberal world has been like.[1]

The crucial point of which people here are still so little aware is, however, not merely the magnitude of the changes which have taken place during the last generation, but the fact that they mean

[1] Even in that year the Macmillan Report could speak already of " the change of outlook of the government of this country in recent, times, its growing pre-occupation, irrespective of party, with the management of the life of the people " and add that " Parliament finds itself increasingly engaged in legislation which has for its conscious aim the regulation of the day-to-day affairs of the community and now intervenes in matters formerly thought to be entirely outside its scope ". This could be said before, later in the same year, the country finally took the headlong plunge and, in the short space of the inglorious years 1931 to 1939, transformed its economic system beyond recognition.

a complete change in the direction of the evolution of our ideas and social order.   For at least twenty-five years before the spectre of totalitarianism became a real threat, we had progressively been moving away from the basic ideas on which European civilisation has been built.   That this movement on which we have entered with such high hopes and ambitions should have brought us face to face with the totalitarian horror has come as a profound shock to this generation, which still refuses to connect the two facts.   Yet this development merely confirms the warnings of the fathers of the liberal philosophy which we still profess.   We have progressively abandoned that freedom in economic affairs without which personal and political freedom has never existed in the past.   Although we had been warned by some of the greatest political thinkers of the nineteenth century, by de Tocqueville and Lord Acton, that socialism means slavery, we have steadily moved in the direction of socialism.   And now that we have seen a new form of slavery arise before our eyes, we have so completely forgotten the warning, that it scarcely occurs to us that the two things may be connected.[1]

How sharp a break not only with the recent past but with the whole evolution of Western civilisation the modern trend towards socialism means, becomes clear if we consider it not merely against the background of the nineteenth century, but in a longer historical perspective.   We are rapidly abandoning not the views merely of Cobden and Bright, of Adam Smith and Hume, or even of Locke and Milton, but one of the salient characteristics of Western civilisation as it has grown from the foundations laid by Christianity and the Greeks and Romans. Not merely nineteenth- and eighteenth-century liberalism, but the basic individualism inherited by us from Erasmus and Montaigne, from Cicero and Tacitus, Pericles and Thucydides is progressively relinquished.

The Nazi leader who described the National-Socialist revolution as a counter-Renaissance spoke more truly than he probably knew.   It was the decisive step in the destruction of that civilisation which modern man had built up from the age of the Renaissance and which was above all an individualist civilisation. Individualism has a bad name to-day and the term has come to be connected with egotism and selfishness.   But the individualism of which we speak in contrast to socialism and all other forms

---

[1] Even much more recent warnings which have proved dreadfully true have been almost entirely forgotten.   It is not yet thirty years since Mr. Hilaire Belloc, in a book which explains more of what has happened since in Germany than most works written after the event, explained that " the effect of Socialist doctrine on Capitalist society is to produce a third thing different from either of its two begetters—to wit, the Servile State " (*The Servile State*, 1913, 3rd ed. 1927, p. xiv).

of collectivism has no necessary connection with these. Only gradually in the course of this book shall we be able to make clear the contrast between the two opposing principles. But the essential features of that individualism which, from elements provided by Christianity and the philosophy of classical antiquity, was first fully developed during the Renaissance and has since grown and spread into what we know as Western European civilisation—the respect for the individual man *qua* man, that is the recognition of his own views and tastes as supreme in his own sphere, however narrowly that may be circumscribed, and the belief that it is desirable that men should develop their own individual gifts and bents. " Freedom " and " liberty " are now words so worn with use and abuse that one must hesitate to employ them to express the ideals for which they stood during that period. Tolerance is, perhaps, the only word which still preserves the full meaning of the principle which during the whole of this period was in the ascendant and which only in recent times has again been in decline, to disappear completely with the rise of the totalitarian state.

The gradual transformation of a rigidly organised hierarchic system into one where men could at least attempt to shape their own life, where man gained the opportunity of knowing and choosing between different forms of life, is closely associated with the growth of commerce. From the commercial cities of Northern Italy the new view of life spread with commerce to the west and north, through France and the south-west of Germany to the Low Countries and the British Isles, taking firm root wherever there was no despotic political power to stifle it. In the Low Countries and Britain it for a long time enjoyed its fullest development and for the first time had an opportunity to grow freely and to become the foundation of the social and political life of these countries. And it was from there that in the late seventeenth and eighteenth centuries it again began to spread in a more fully developed form to the West and East, to the New World and the centre of the European continent where devastating wars and political oppression had largely submerged the earlier beginnings of a similar growth.[1]

During the whole of this modern period of European history the general direction of social development was one of freeing the individual from the ties which had bound him to the customary or prescribed ways in the pursuit of his ordinary activities. The conscious realisation that the spontaneous and uncontrolled efforts of individuals were capable of producing a complex order of

[1] The most fateful of these developments, pregnant with consequences not yet extinct, was the subjection and partial destruction of the German bourgeoisie by the territorial princes in the fifteenth and sixteenth centuries

economic activities could come only after this development had made some progress. The subsequent elaboration of a consistent argument in favour of economic freedom was the outcome of a free growth of economic activity which had been the undesigned and unforeseen by-product of political freedom.

Perhaps the greatest result of the unchaining of individual energies was the marvellous growth of science which followed the march of individual liberty from Italy to England and beyond. That the inventive faculty of man had been no less in earlier periods is shown by the many highly ingenious automatic toys and other mechanical contrivances constructed while industrial technique still remained stationary, and by the development in some industries which, like mining or watch-making, were not subject to restrictive controls. But the few attempts towards a more extended industrial use of mechanical inventions, some extraordinarily advanced, were promptly suppressed, and the desire for knowledge was stifled, so long as the dominant views were held to be binding for all : the beliefs of the great majority on what was right and proper were allowed to bar the way of the individual innovator. Only since industrial freedom opened the path to the free use of new knowledge, only since everything could be tried—if somebody could be found to back it at his own risk—and, it should be added, as often as not from outside the authorities officially entrusted with the cultivation of learning, has science made the great strides which in the last hundred and fifty years have changed the face of the world.

As is so often true, the nature of our civilisation has been seen more clearly by its enemies than by most of its friends : " the perennial Western malady, the revolt of the individual against the species ", as that nineteenth-century totalitarian, Auguste Comte, has described it, was indeed the force which built our civilisation. What the nineteenth century added to the individualism of the preceding period was merely to make all classes conscious of freedom, to develop systematically and continuously what had grown in a haphazard and patchy manner and to spread it from England and Holland over most of the European Continent.

The result of this growth surpassed all expectations. Wherever the barriers to the free exercise of human ingenuity were removed man became rapidly able to satisfy ever-widening ranges of desire. And while the rising standard soon led to the discovery of very dark spots in society, spots which men were no longer willing to tolerate, there was probably no class that did not substantially benefit from the general advance. We cannot do justice to this astonishing growth if we measure it by our present standards, which themselves result from this growth and now make many defects obvious. To appreciate what it meant to those who took part in it we must measure it by the hopes and wishes men held when it began : and there can be no doubt that its success surpassed man's wildest dreams, that by the beginning of the twentieth century the working man in the Western world had reached a degree of material comfort, security, and personal independence which a hundred years before had seemed scarcely possible.

What in the future will probably appear the most significant and far-reaching effect of this success is the new sense of power over their own fate, the belief in the unbounded possibilities of improving their own lot, which the success already achieved created among men. With the success grew ambition—and man had every right to be ambitious. What had been an inspiring promise seemed no longer enough, the rate of progress far too slow ; and the principles which had made this progress possible in the past came to be regarded more as obstacles to speedier progress, impatiently to be brushed away, than as the conditions for the preservation and development of what had already been achieved.

* * * * *

There is nothing in the basic principles of liberalism to make it a stationary creed, there are no hard-and-fast rules fixed once and for all. The fundamental principle that in the ordering of our affairs we should make as much use as possible of the spontaneous forces of society, and resort as little as possible to coercion, is capable of an infinite variety of applications. There is, in particular, all the difference between deliberately creating a system within which competition will work as beneficially as possible, and passively accepting institutions as they are. Probably nothing has done so much harm to the liberal cause as the wooden insistence of some liberals on certain rough rules of thumb, above all the principle of *laissez-faire*. Yet in a sense this was necessary and unavoidable. Against the innumerable interests who could show that particular measures would confer immediate and obvious benefits on some, while the harm they caused was much more indirect and difficult to see, nothing short of some hard-and-fast rule would have been effective. And since a strong presumption in favour of industrial liberty had undoubtedly been established, the temptation to present it as a rule which knew no exceptions was too strong always to be resisted.

But with this attitude taken by many popularisers of the liberal doctrine, it was almost inevitable that, once their position was penetrated at some points, it should soon collapse as a whole. The position was further weakened by the inevitably slow progress of a policy which aimed at a gradual improvement of the institutional framework of a free society. This progress depended on the growth of our understanding of the social forces and the conditions most favourable to their working in a desirable manner. Since the task was to assist, and where necessary to supplement, their operation, the first requisite was to understand them. The attitude of the liberal towards society is like that of the gardener who tends a plant and in order to create the conditions most favourable to its growth must know as much as possible about its structure and the way it functions.

No sensible person should have doubted that the crude rules in which the principles of economic policy of the nineteenth century were expressed were only a beginning, that we had yet much to learn, and that there were still immense possibilities of advancement on the lines on which we had moved. But this advance could only come as we gained increasing intellectual mastery of the forces of which we had to make use. There were many obvious tasks, such as our handling of the monetary system, and the prevention or control of monopoly, and an even greater number of less obvious but hardly less important tasks to be undertaken in other fields, where there could be no doubt that the governments possessed enormous powers for good and evil ; and there was every reason to expect that with a better understanding of the problems we should some day be able to use these powers successfully.

But while the progress towards what is commonly called " positive " action was necessarily slow, and while for the immediate improvement liberalism had to rely largely on the gradual increase of wealth which freedom brought about, it had constantly to fight proposals which threatened this progress. It came to be regarded as a " negative " creed because it could offer to particular individuals little more than a share in the common progress—a progress which came to be taken more and more for granted and was no longer recognised as the result of the policy of freedom. It might even be said that the very success of liberalism became the cause of its decline. Because of the success already achieved man became increasingly unwilling to tolerate the evils still with him which now appeared both unbearable and unnecessary.

*　　*　　*　　*　　*

Because of the growing impatience with the slow advance of liberal policy, the just irritation with those who used liberal phraseology in defence of anti-social privileges, and the boundless ambition seemingly justified by the material improvements already achieved, it came to pass that toward the turn of the century the belief in the basic tenets of liberalism was more and more relinquished. What had been achieved came to be regarded as a secure and imperishable possession, acquired once and for all. The eyes of the people became fixed on the new demands, the rapid satisfaction of which seemed to be barred by the adherence to the old principles. It became more and more widely accepted that further advance could not be expected along the old lines within the general framework which had made past progress possible, but only by a complete remodelling of society. It was no longer a question of adding to or improving the existing machinery, but of completely scrapping and replacing it. And as the hope of the new generation came to be centred on something completely new, interest in, and understanding of, the functioning of the existing society rapidly declined; and with the decline of the understanding of the way in which the free system worked our awareness of what depended on its existence also decreased.

This is not the place to discuss how this change in outlook was fostered by the uncritical transfer to the problems of society of habits of thought engendered by the preoccupation with technological problems, the habits of thought of the natural scientist and the engineer, how these at the same time tended to discredit the results of the past study of society which did not conform to their prejudices, and to impose ideals of organisation on a sphere to which they are not appropriate.[1] All we are here concerned to show is how completely, though gradually and by almost imperceptible steps, our attitude towards society has changed. What at every stage of this process of change had appeared a difference of degree only, has in its cumulative effect already brought about a fundamental difference between the older liberal attitude towards society and the present approach to social problems. The change amounts to a complete reversal of the trend we have sketched, an entire abandonment of the individualist tradition which has created Western civilisation.

According to the views now dominant the question is no longer how we can make the best use of the spontaneous forces found in a free society. We have in effect undertaken to dispense with the forces which produced unforeseen results and to replace the impersonal and anonymous mechanism of the market by collective and " conscious " direction of all social forces to deliberately chosen goals. The difference cannot be better illustrated than by the extreme position taken in a widely acclaimed

---

[1] The author has made an attempt to trace the beginning of this development in two series of articles on " Scientism and the Study of Society " and " The Counter-Revolution of Science " which appeared in *Economica*, 1941-4.

book on whose programme of so-called " planning for freedom "
we shall have to comment yet more than once.

> We have never had to set up and direct [writes Dr. Karl Mannheim]
> the entire system of nature as we are forced to do to-day with society.
> . . . Mankind is tending more and more to regulate the whole of
> its social life, although it has never attempted to create a second
> nature.[1]

*   *   *   *   *

It is significant that this change in the trend of ideas has
coincided with a reversal of the direction in which ideas have
travelled in space. For over two hundred years English ideas
had been spreading eastwards. The rule of freedom which had
been achieved in England seemed destined to spread throughout
the world. By about 1870 the reign of these ideas had probably
reached its easternmost expansion. From then onwards it began
to retreat and a different set of ideas, not really new but very old,
began to advance from the East. England lost her intellectual
leadership in the political and social sphere and became an
importer of ideas. For the next sixty years Germany became
the centre from which the ideas destined to govern the world
in the twentieth century spread east and west. Whether it was
Hegel or Marx, List or Schmoller, Sombart or Mannheim,
whether it was socialism in its more radical form or merely
" organisation " or " planning " of a less radical kind, German
ideas were everywhere readily imported and German institutions
imitated. Although most of the new ideas, and particularly
socialism, did not originate in Germany, it was in Germany that
they were perfected and during the last quarter of the nineteenth
and the first quarter of the twentieth century they reached their
fullest development. It is now often forgotten how very considerable was the lead which Germany had during this period
in the development of the theory and practice of socialism,
that a generation before socialism became a serious issue in this
country, Germany had a large socialist party in her parliament,
and that till not very long ago the doctrinal development of
socialism was almost entirely carried on in Germany and Austria,
so that even to-day Russian discussion largely carries on where
the Germans left off ; most English socialists are still unaware
that the majority of the problems they begin to discover were
thoroughly discussed by German socialists long ago.

The intellectual influence which German thinkers were able
to exercise during this period on the whole world was supported
not merely by the great material progress of Germany but even
more by the extraordinary reputation which German thinkers and

[1] *Man and Society in an Age of Reconstruction*, 1940, p. 175.

scientists had earned during the preceding hundred years when Germany had once more become an integral and even leading member of the common European civilisation. But it soon served to assist the spreading from Germany of ideas directed against the foundations of that civilisation. The Germans themselves— or at least those among them who spread these ideas—were fully aware of the conflict : what had been the common heritage of European civilisation became to them, long before the Nazis, " Western " civilisation—where " Western " was no longer used in the old sense of Occident but had come to mean west of the Rhine. " Western " in this sense was Liberalism and Democracy, Capitalism and Individualism, Free Trade and any form of Internationalism or love of peace.

But in spite of the ill-concealed contempt of an ever-increasing number of Germans for those " shallow " Western ideals, or perhaps because of it, the people of the West continued to import German ideas and were even induced to believe that their own former convictions had merely been rationalisations of selfish interests, that Free Trade was a doctrine invented to further British interests, and that the political ideals England had given to the world were hopelessly outmoded and a thing to be ashamed of.

CHAPTER II

THE GREAT UTOPIA

What has always made the state a hell on earth has been
precisely that man has tried to make it his heaven.

F. Hoelderlin.

THAT socialism has displaced liberalism as the doctrine held
by the great majority of progressives does not simply mean that
people had forgotten the warnings of the great liberal thinkers of
the past about the consequences of collectivism. It has happened
because they were persuaded of the very opposite of what these
men had predicted. The extraordinary thing is that the same
socialism that was not only early recognised as the gravest
threat to freedom, but quite openly began as a reaction against
the liberalism of the French Revolution, gained general acceptance under the flag of liberty. It is rarely remembered now
that socialism in its beginnings was frankly authoritarian.
The French writers who laid the foundations of modern
socialism had no doubt that their ideas could be put into
practice only by a strong dictatorial government. To them
socialism meant an attempt to " terminate the revolution "
by a deliberate reorganisation of society on hierarchical lines,
and the imposition of a coercive " spiritual power ". Where
freedom was concerned, the founders of socialism made no bones
about their intentions. Freedom of thought they regarded as the
root-evil of nineteenth-century society, and the first of modern
planners, Saint-Simon, even predicted that those who did not
obey his proposed planning boards would be " treated as cattle ".

Only under the influence of the strong democratic currents
preceding the revolution of 1848 did socialism begin to ally
itself with the forces of freedom. But it took the new " democratic
socialism " a long time to live down the suspicions aroused by
its antecedents. Nobody saw more clearly than de Tocqueville
that democracy as an essentially individualist institution stood
in an irreconcilable conflict with socialism :

> Democracy extends the sphere of individual freedom [he said in
> 1848], socialism restricts it. Democracy attaches all possible value
> to each man ; socialism makes each man a mere agent, a mere num-
> ber. Democracy and socialism have nothing in common but one
> word : equality. But notice the difference : while democracy seeks
> equality in liberty, socialism seeks equality in restraint and servitude.[1]

[1] " Discours prononcé à l'assemblée constituante le 12 Septembre 1848 sur
la question du droit au travail." *Œuvres complètes d'Alexis de Tocqueville*,
vol. IX, 1866, p. 546.

18

To allay these suspicions and to harness to its cart the strongest of all political motives, the craving for freedom, socialism began increasingly to make use of the promise of a " new freedom ". The coming of socialism was to be the leap from the realm of necessity to the realm of freedom. It was to bring " economic freedom ", without which the political freedom already gained was " not worth having ". Only socialism was capable of effecting the consummation of the agelong struggle for freedom in which the attainment of political freedom was but a first step.

The subtle change in meaning to which the word freedom was subjected in order that this argument should sound plausible is important. To the great apostles of political freedom the word had meant freedom from coercion, freedom from the arbitrary power of other men, release from the ties which left the individual no choice but obedience to the orders of a superior to whom he was attached. The new freedom promised, however, was to be freedom from necessity, release from the compulsion of the circumstances which inevitably limit the range of choice of all of us, although for some very much more than for others. Before man could be truly free, the " despotism of physical want " had to be broken, the " restraints of the economic system " relaxed.

Freedom in this sense is, of course, merely another name for power [1] or wealth. Yet, although the promises of this new freedom were often coupled with irresponsible promises of a great increase in material wealth in a socialist society, it was not from such an absolute conquest of the niggardliness of nature that economic freedom was expected. What the promise really amounted to was that the great existing disparities in the range of choice of different people were to disappear. The demand for the new freedom was thus only another name for the old demand for an equal distribution of wealth. But the new name gave the socialists another word in common with the liberals and they exploited it to the full. And although the word was used in a different sense by the two groups, few people noticed this and still fewer asked themselves whether the two kinds of freedom promised really could be combined.

[1] The characteristic confusion of freedom with power, which we shall meet again and again throughout this discussion, is too big a subject to be thoroughly examined here. As old as socialism itself, it is so closely allied with it that almost seventy years ago a French scholar, discussing its Saint-Simonian origins, was led to say that this theory of liberty " est à elle seule tout le socialisme " (P. Janet, *Saint-Simon et le Saint-Simonisme*, 1878, p. 26, note). The most explicit defender of this confusion is, significantly, the leading philosopher of American left-wingism, John Dewey, according to whom " liberty is the effective power to do specific things " so that " the demand for liberty is demand for power " (" Liberty and Social Control ", *The Social Frontier*, November 1935, p. 41).

There can be no doubt that the promise of greater freedom has become one of the most effective weapons of socialist propaganda and that the belief that socialism would bring freedom is genuine and sincere. But this would only heighten the tragedy if it should prove that what was promised to us as the Road to Freedom was in fact the High Road to Servitude. Unquestionably the promise of more freedom was responsible for luring more and more liberals along the socialist road, for blinding them to the conflict which exists between the basic principles of socialism and liberalism, and for often enabling socialists to usurp the very name of the old party of freedom. Socialism was embraced by the greater part of the intelligentsia as the apparent heir of the liberal tradition : therefore it is not surprising that to them the idea should appear inconceivable of socialism leading to the opposite of liberty.

*   *   *   *   *

In recent years, however, the old apprehensions of the unforeseen consequences of socialism have once more been strongly voiced from the most unexpected quarters. Observer after observer, in spite of the contrary expectation with which he approached his subject, has been impressed with the extraordinary similarity in many respects of the conditions under " fascism " and " communism ". While " progressives " in this country and elsewhere wére still deluding themselves that communism and fascism represented opposite poles, more and more people began to ask themselves whether these new tyrannies were not the outcome of the same tendencies. Even communists must have been somewhat shaken by such testimonies as that of Mr. Max Eastman, Lenin's old friend, who found himself compelled to admit that " instead of being better, Stalinism is worse than fascism, more ruthless, barbarous, unjust, immoral, anti-democratic, unredeemed by any hope or scruple ", and that it is " better described as superfascist " ; and when we find the same author recognising that " Stalinism *is* socialism, in the sense of being an inevitable although unforeseen political accompaniment of the nationalisation and collectivisation which he had relied upon as part of his plan for erecting a classless society ",[1] his conclusion clearly achieves wider significance.

Mr. Eastman's case is perhaps the most remarkable, yet he is by no means the first or the only sympathetic observer of the Russian experiment to form similar conclusions. Several years earlier Mr. W. H. Chamberlin, who in twelve years in Russia as an American correspondent had seen all his ideals shattered, summed up the conclusions of his studies there and

[1] Max Eastman, *Stalin's Russia and the Crisis of Socialism*, 1940, p. 82.

in Germany and Italy in the statement that " Socialism is certain
to prove, in the beginning at least, the road NOT to freedom,
but to dictatorship and counter-dictatorships, to civil war of the
fiercest kind. Socialism achieved and maintained by democratic
means seems definitely to belong to the world of utopias." [1]
Similarly a British writer, Mr. F. A. Voigt, after many years of
close observation of developments in Europe as a foreign correspondent, concludes that " Marxism has led to Fascism and
National-Socialism, because, in all essentials, it is Fascism and
National Socialism " [2] And Dr. Walter Lippmann has arrived
at the conviction that

the generation to which we belong is now learning from experience
what happens when men retreat from freedom to a coercive organisation of their affairs. Though they promise themselves a more
abundant life, they must in practice renounce it ; as the organised
direction increases, the variety of ends must give way to uniformity.
That is the nemesis of the planned society and the authoritarian
principle in human affairs.[3]

Many more similar statements from people in a position to
judge might be selected from publications of recent years, particularly from those by men who as citizens of the now totalitarian
countries have lived through the transformation and have been
forced by their experience to revise many cherished beliefs. We
shall quote as one more example a German writer who expresses the same conclusion perhaps more justly than those already
quoted.

The complete collapse of the belief in the attainability of freedom
and equality through Marxism [writes Mr. Peter Drucker [4]] has
forced Russia to travel the same road towards a totalitarian,
purely negative, non-economic society of unfreedom and inequality
which Germany has been following. Not that communism and
fascism are essentially the same. Fascism is the stage reached after
communism has proved an illusion, and it has proved as much an
illusion in Stalinist Russia as in pre-Hitler Germany.

No less significant is the intellectual history of many of the
Nazi and Fascist leaders. Everybody who has watched the
growth of these movements in Italy [5] or Germany has been
struck by the number of leading men, from Mussolini downwards
(and not excluding Laval and Quisling), who began as socialists

[1] W. H. Chamberlin, *A False Utopia*, 1937, p. 202-3.
[2] F. A. Voigt, *Unto Cæsar*, 1939, p. 95.
[3] *Atlantic Monthly*, November 1936, p. 552.
[4] *The End of Economic Man*, 1939, p. 230.
[5] An illuminating account of the intellectual history of many of the Fascist
leaders will be found in R. Michels (himself an ex-Marxist Fascist), *Sozialismus
und Faszismus*, Munich 1925, vol. II, pp. 264-6, and 311-12.

and ended as Fascists or Nazis. And what is true of the leaders is even more true of the rank and file of the movement. The relative ease with which a young communist could be converted into a Nazi or *vice versa* was generally known in Germany, best of all to the propagandists of the two parties. Many a University teacher in this country during the 1930's has seen English and American students return from the Continent, uncertain whether they were communists or Nazis and certain only that they hated Western liberal civilisation.

It is true, of course, that in Germany before 1933 and in Italy before 1922 communists and Nazis or Fascists clashed more frequently with each other than with other parties. They competed for the support of the same type of mind and reserved for each other the hatred of the heretic. But their practice showed how closely they are related. To both, the real enemy, the man with whom they had nothing in common and whom they could not hope to convince, is the liberal of the old type. While to the Nazi the communist, and to the communist the Nazi, and to both the socialist, are potential recruits who are made of the right timber, although they have listened to false prophets, they both know that there can be no compromise between them and those who really believe in individual freedom.

Lest this be doubted by people misled by official propaganda from either side, let me quote one more statement from an authority that ought not to be suspect. In an article under the significant title of " The Rediscovery of Liberalism ", Professor Eduard Heimann, one of the leaders of German religious socialism, writes :

> Hitlerism proclaims itself as both true democracy and true socialism, and the terrible truth is that there is a grain of truth for such claims—an infinitesimal grain, to be sure, but at any rate enough to serve as a basis for such fantastic distortions. Hitlerism even goes so far as to claim the rôle of protector of Christianity, and the terrible truth is that even this gross misinterpretation is able to make some impression. But one fact stands out with perfect clarity in all the fog : Hitler has never claimed to represent true liberalism. Liberalism then has the distinction of being the doctrine most hated by Hitler.[1]

It should be added that this hatred had little occasion to show itself in practice merely because, by the time Hitler came to

[1] *Social Research* (New York), vol. VIII, no. 4, November 1941.—It deserves to be recalled in this connection that, whatever may have been his reasons, Hitler thought it expedient to declare in one of his public speeches as late as February 1941 that " basically National Socialism and Marxism are the same " (Cf. *The Bulletin of International News* published by the Royal Institute of International Affairs, vol. XVIII, no. 5, p. 269.)

power, liberalism was to all intents and purposes dead in Germany. And it was socialism that had killed it.

*   *   *   *   *

While to many who have watched the transition from socialism to fascism at close quarters the connection between the two systems has become increasingly obvious, in this country the majority of people still believe that socialism and freedom can be combined. There can be no doubt that most socialists here still believe profoundly in the liberal ideal of freedom, and that they would recoil if they became convinced that the realisation of their programme would mean the destruction of freedom. So little is the problem yet seen, so easily do the most irreconcilable ideals still live together, that we can still hear such contradictions in terms as " individualist socialism " seriously discussed. If this is the state of mind which makes us drift into a new world, nothing can be more urgent than that we should seriously examine the real significance of the evolution that has taken place elsewhere. Although our conclusions will only confirm the apprehensions which others have already expressed, the reasons why this development cannot be regarded as accidental will not appear without a rather full examination of the main aspects of this transformation of social life. That democratic socialism, the great utopia of the last few generations, is not only unachievable, but that to strive for it produces something so utterly different that few of those who now wish it would be prepared to accept the consequences, many will not believe till the connection has been laid bare in all its aspects.

CHAPTER III

INDIVIDUALISM AND COLLECTIVISM

> The socialists believe in two things which are absolutely different and perhaps even contradictory : freedom and organisation.
>
> *Elie Halévy.*

BEFORE we can progress with our main problem, an obstacle has yet to be surmounted. A confusion largely responsible for the way in which we are drifting into things which nobody wants must be cleared up.

This confusion concerns nothing less than the concept of socialism itself. It may mean, and is often used to describe, merely the ideals of social justice, greater equality and security which are the ultimate aims of socialism. But it means also the particular method by which most socialists hope to attain these ends and which many competent people regard as the only methods by which they can be fully and quickly attained. In this sense socialism means the abolition of private enterprise, of private ownership of the means of production, and the creation of a system of " planned economy " in which the entrepreneur working for profit is replaced by a central planning body.

There are many people who call themselves socialists although they care only about the first, who fervently believe in those ultimate aims of socialism but neither care nor understand how they can be achieved, and who are merely certain that they must be achieved, whatever the cost. But to nearly all those to whom socialism is not merely a hope but an object of practical politics, the characteristic methods of modern socialism are as essential as the ends themselves. Many people, on the other hand, who value the ultimate ends of socialism no less than the socialists, refuse to support socialism because of the dangers to other values they see in the methods proposed by the socialists. The dispute about socialism has thus become largely a dispute about means and not about ends—although the question whether the different ends of socialism can be simultaneously achieved is also involved.

This would be enough to create confusion. And the confusion has been further increased by the common practice of denying that those who repudiate the means value the ends. But this is not all. The situation is still more complicated by the fact that the same means, the " economic planning " which is the prime instrument of socialist reform, can be used for many other

24

purposes. We must centrally direct economic activity if we want to make the distribution of income conform to current ideas of social justice. " Planning ", therefore, is wanted by all those who demand that " production for use " be substituted for production for profit. But such planning is no less indispensable if the distribution of incomes is to be regulated in a way which to us appears to be the opposite of just. Whether we should wish that more of the good things of this world should go to some racial élite, the Nordic men, or the members of a party or an aristocracy, the methods which we shall have to employ are the same as those which could ensure an equalitarian distribution.

It may, perhaps, seem unfair to use the term socialism to describe its methods rather than its aims, to use for a particular method a term which for many people stands for an ultimate ideal. It is probably preferable to describe the methods which can be used for a great variety of ends as collectivism and to regard socialism as a species of that genus. Yet, although to most socialists only one species of collectivism will represent true socialism, it must always be remembered that socialism is a species of collectivism and that therefore everything which is true of collectivism as such must apply also to socialism. Nearly all the points which are disputed between socialists and liberals concern the methods common to all forms of collectivism and not the particular ends for which socialists want to use them ; and all the consequences with which we shall be concerned in this book follow from the methods of collectivism irrespective of the ends for which they are used. It must also not be forgotten that socialism is not only by far the most important species of collectivism or " planning " ; but that it is socialism which has persuaded liberal-minded people to submit once more to that regimentation of economic life which they had overthrown because, in the words of Adam Smith, it puts governments in a position where " to support themselves they are obliged to be oppressive and tyrannical ".[1]

*   *   *   *   *

The difficulties caused by the ambiguities of the common political terms are not yet over if we agree to use the term collectivism so as to include all types of " planned economy ", whatever the end of planning. The meaning of this term becomes somewhat more definite if we make it clear that we mean that sort of planning which is necessary to realise any given distributive ideals. But as the idea of central economic planning owes its appeal largely to this very vagueness of its meaning, it is

---

[1] Quoted in Dugald Stewart's *Memoir of Adam Smith* from a memorandum written by Smith in 1755.

essential that we should agree on its precise sense before we discuss its consequences.

" Planning " owes its popularity largely to the fact that everybody desires, of course, that we should handle our common problems as rationally as possible, and that in so doing we should use as much foresight as we can command. In this sense everybody who is not a complete fatalist is a planner, every political act is (or ought to be) an act of planning, and there can be differences only between good and bad, between wise and foresighted and foolish and short-sighted planning. An economist, whose whole task is the study of how men actually do and how they might plan their affairs, is the last person who could object to planning in this general sense. But it is not in this sense that our enthusiasts for a planned society now employ this term, nor merely in this sense that we must plan if we want the distribution of income or wealth to conform to some particular standard. According to the modern planners, and for their purposes, it is not sufficient to design the most rational permanent framework within which the various activities would be conducted by different persons according to their individual plans. This liberal plan, according to them, is no plan—and it is indeed not a plan designed to satisfy particular views about who should have what. What our planners demand is a central direction of all economic activity according to a single plan, laying down how the resources of society should be " consciously directed " to serve particular ends in a definite way.

The dispute between the modern planners and their opponents is, therefore, *not* a dispute on whether we ought to choose intelligently between the various possible organisations of society ; it is not a dispute on whether we ought to employ foresight and systematic thinking in planning our common affairs. It is a dispute about what is the best way of so doing. The question is whether for this purpose it is better that the holder of coercive power should confine himself in general to creating conditions under which the knowledge and initiative of individuals is given the best scope so that *they* can plan most successfully ; or whether a rational utilisation of our resources requires *central* direction and organisation of all our activities according to some consciously constructed " blueprint ". The socialists of all parties have appropriated the term planning for planning of the latter type and it is now generally accepted in this sense. But though this is meant to suggest that this is the only rational way of handling our affairs, it does not of course prove this. It remains the point on which the planners and the liberals disagree.

* * * * *

It is important not to confuse opposition against this kind of planning with a dogmatic *laissez-faire* attitude. The liberal argument is in favour of making the best possible use of the forces of competition as a means of co-ordinating human efforts, not an argument for leaving things just as they are. It is based on the conviction that where effective competition can be created, it is a better way of guiding individual efforts than any other. It does not deny, but even emphasises, that, in order that competition should work beneficially, a carefully thought-out legal framework is required, and that neither the existing nor the past legal rules are free from grave defects. Nor does it deny that where it is impossible to create the conditions necessary to make competition effective, we must resort to other methods of guiding economic activity. Economic liberalism is opposed, however, to competition being supplanted by inferior methods of co-ordinating individual efforts. And it regards competition as superior not only because it is in most circumstances the most efficient method known, but even more because it is the only method by which our activities can be adjusted to each other without coercive or arbitrary intervention of authority. Indeed, one of the main arguments in favour of competition is that it dispenses with the need for " conscious social control " and that it gives the individuals a chance to decide whether the prospects of a particular occupation are sufficient to compensate for the disadvantages and risks connected with it.

The successful use of competition as the principle of social organisation precludes certain types of coercive interference with economic life, but it admits of others which sometimes may very considerably assist its work and even requires certain kinds of government action. But there is good reason why the negative requirements, the points where coercion must not be used, have been particularly stressed. It is necessary in the first instance that the parties in the market should be free to sell and buy at any price at which they can find a partner to the transaction, and that anybody should be free to produce, sell, and buy anything that may be produced or sold at all. And it is essential that the entry into the different trades should be open to all on equal terms, and that the law should not tolerate any attempts by individuals or groups to restrict this entry by open or concealed force. Any attempt to control prices or quantities of particular commodities deprives competition of its power of bringing about an effective co-ordination of individual efforts, because price changes then cease to register all the relevant changes in circumstances and no longer provide a reliable guide for the individual's actions.

This is not necessarily true, however, of measures merely

restricting the allowed methods of production, so long as these restrictions affect all potential producers equally and are not used as an indirect way of controlling prices and quantities. Though all such controls of the methods or production impose extra costs, i.e. make it necessary to use more resources to produce a given output, they may be well worth while. To prohibit the use of certain poisonous substances, or to require special precautions in their use, to limit working hours or to require certain sanitary arrangements, is fully compatible with the preservation of competition. The only question here is whether in the particular instance the advantages gained are greater than the social costs which they impose. Nor is the preservation of competition incompatible with an extensive system of social services—so long as the organisation of these services is not designed in such a way as to make competition ineffective over wide fields.

It is regrettable, though not difficult to explain, that much less attention than to these negative points has in the past been given to the positive requirements of a successful working of the competitive system. The functioning of competition not only requires adequate organisation of certain institutions like money, markets, and channels of information—some of which can never be adequately provided by private enterprise—but it depends above all on the existence of an appropriate legal system, a legal system designed both to preserve competition and to make it operate as beneficially as possible. It is by no means sufficient that the law should recognise the principle of private property and freedom of contract ; much depends on the precise definition of the right of property as applied to different things. The systematic study of the forms of legal institutions which will make the competitive system work efficiently has been sadly neglected ; and strong arguments can be advanced that serious shortcomings here, particularly with regard to the law of corporations and of patents, have not only made competition work much more badly than it might have done, but have even led to the destruction of competition in many spheres.

There are, finally, undoubted fields where no legal arrangements can create the main condition on which the usefulness of the system of competition and private property depends : namely, that the owner benefits from all the useful services rendered by his property and suffers for all the damages caused to others by its use. Where, for example, it is impracticable to make the enjoyment of certain services dependent on the payment of a price, competition will not produce the services ; and the price system becomes similarly ineffective when the damage caused to others by certain uses of property cannot be effectively charged to the owner of that property. In all these instances there is a divergence between the items which enter into private calculation and those which affect social welfare ; and whenever this divergence becomes important some method other than competition may have to be found to supply the services in question. Thus neither the provision of signposts on the roads, nor, in most circumstances, that of the roads themselves, can be paid for by every individual user. Nor can certain harmful effects of deforestation, or of some methods of farming, or of the smoke and noise of factories, be confined to the owner of the property in question or to those who are willing to submit to the damage for an agreed compensation. In such instances we must find some substitute for the regulation by the price mechanism. But the fact that we have to resort to the substitution of direct regulation by authority where the conditions for the proper working of competition cannot be created, does not prove that we should suppress competition where it can be made to function.

To create conditions in which competition will be as effective as possible, to supplement it where it cannot be made effective, to provide the services which, in the words of Adam Smith, " though they may be in the highest degree advantageous to a great society, are, however, of such a nature, that the profit could never repay the expense to any individual or small number of individuals ", these tasks provide indeed a wide and unquestioned field for state activity. In no system that could be rationally defended would the state just do nothing. An effective competitive system needs an intelligently designed and continuously adjusted legal framework as much as any other. Even the most essential prerequisite of its proper functioning, the prevention of fraud and deception (including exploitation of ignorance) provides a great and by no means yet fully accomplished object of legislative activity.

* * * * *

The task of creating a suitable framework for the beneficial working of competition had, however, not yet been carried very far when states everywhere turned from it to that of supplanting competition by a different and irreconcilable principle. The question was no longer one of making competition work and of supplementing it, but of displacing it altogether. It is important to be quite clear about this : the modern movement for planning is a movement against competition as such, a new flag under which all the old enemies of competition have rallied. And although all sorts of interests are now trying to re-establish under this flag privileges which the liberal era swept away, it is socialist propaganda for planning which has restored to respectability among liberal-minded people opposition to competition, and which has effectively lulled the healthy suspicion which any attempt to smother competition used to arouse.[1] What in effect unites the socialists of the Left and the Right is this common hostility to competition and their common desire to replace it by a directed economy. Though the terms capitalism and socialism are still generally used to describe the past and the future forms of society, they conceal rather than elucidate the nature of the transition through which we are passing.

Yet, though all the changes we are observing tend in the direction of a comprehensive central direction of economic activity, the universal struggle against competition promises to produce in the first instance something in many respects even worse, a state of affairs which can satisfy neither planners nor liberals : a sort of syndicalist or " corporative " organisation of industry, in which competition is more or less suppressed but planning is left in the hands of the independent monopolies of the separate industries. This is the inevitable first result of a situation in which the people are united in their hostility to competition but agree on little else. By destroying competition in industry after industry, this policy puts the consumer at the mercy of the joint monopolist action of capitalists and workers in the best organised industries. Yet, although this is a state of affairs which in wide fields has already existed for some time, and although much of the muddled (and most of the interested) agitation for planning aims at it, it is not a state which is likely to persist or can be rationally justified. Such independent planning by industrial monopolies would, in fact, produce effects opposite to those at which the argument for planning aims. Once this stage is reached the only alternative to a return to competition is the control of the monopolies by the state, a control which, if it is to be made effective, must become progressively more complete and more detailed. It is this stage we are rapidly approaching. When, shortly before the war, one of the weeklies pointed out that

[1] Of late, it is true, some academic socialists, under the spur of criticism, and animated by the same fear of the extinction of freedom in a centrally planned society, have devised a new kind of " competitive socialism " which they hope will avoid the difficulties and dangers of central planning and combine the abolition of private property with the full retention of individual freedom. Although some discussion of this new kind of socialism has taken place in learned journals, it is hardly likely to recommend itself to practical politicians. If it ever did, it would not be difficult to show (as the author has attempted elsewhere—see *Economica*, 1940) that these plans rest on a delusion and suffer from an inherent contradiction. It is impossible to assume control over all the productive resources without also deciding for whom and by whom they are to be used. Although, under this so-called competitive socialism, the planning by the central authority would take somewhat more roundabout forms, its effects would not be fundamentally different, and the element of competition would be little more than a sham.

" there were many signs that British leaders are growing accustomed to thinking in terms of national development by controlled monopolies ",[1] this was probably a true estimate of the position as it then existed. Since then this process has been greatly accelerated by the war, and its grave defects and dangers will become increasingly obvious as time goes on.

The idea of complete centralisation of the direction of economic activity still appalls most people, not only because of the stupendous difficulty of the task, but even more because of the horror inspired by the idea of everything being directed from a single centre. If we are nevertheless rapidly moving towards such a state this is largely because most people still believe that it must be possible to find some Middle Way between " atomistic " competition and central direction. Nothing indeed seems at first more plausible, or is more likely to appeal to reasonable people, than the idea that our goal must be neither the extreme decentralisation of free competition, nor the complete centralisation of a single plan, but some judicious mixture of the two methods. Yet mere common sense proves a treacherous guide in this field. Although competition can bear some admixture of regulation, it cannot be combined with planning to any extent we like without ceasing to operate as an effective guide to production. Nor is " planning " a medicine which, taken in small doses, can produce the effects for which one might hope from its thoroughgoing application. Both competition and central direction become poor and inefficient tools if they are incomplete ; they are alternative principles used to solve the same problem, and a mixture of the two means that neither will really work and that the result will be worse than if either system had been consistently relied upon. Or, to express it differently, planning and competition can be combined only by planning for competition, but not by planning against competition.

It is of the utmost importance to the argument of this book for the reader to keep in mind that the planning against which all our criticism is directed is solely the planning against competition—the planning which is to be substituted for competition. This is the more important as we cannot, within the scope of this book, enter into a discussion of the very necessary planning which is required to make competition as effective and beneficial as possible. But as in current usage " planning " has become almost synonymous with the former kind of planning, it will sometimes be inevitable for the sake of brevity to refer to it simply as planning, even though this means leaving to our opponents a very good word meriting a better fate.

[1] *The Spectator*, March 3rd, 1939, p. 337.

CHAPTER IV

THE "INEVITABILITY" OF PLANNING

> We were the first to assert that the more complicated the
> forms of civilisation, the more restricted the freedom of the
> individual must become.
>
> *B. Mussolini.*

IT is a revealing fact that few planners are content to say that
central planning is desirable. Most of them affirm that we can
no longer choose but are compelled by circumstances beyond our
control to substitute planning for competition. The myth is
deliberately cultivated that we are embarking on the new course
not out of free will but because competition is spontaneously
eliminated by technological changes which we neither can reverse
nor should wish to prevent. This argument is rarely developed
at any length—it is one of the assertions taken over by one writer
from another till, by mere iteration, it has come to be accepted
as an established fact. It is, nevertheless, devoid of foundation.
The tendency towards monopoly and planning is not the result
of any "objective facts" beyond our control, but the product
of opinions fostered and propagated for half a century till they
have come to dominate all our policy.

Of the various arguments employed to demonstrate the inevitability of planning, the one most frequently heard is that technological changes have made competition impossible in a constantly
increasing number of fields, and that the only choice left to us is
between control of production by private monopolies and direction
by the government. This belief derives mainly from the Marxist
doctrine of the "concentration of industry", although, like so
many Marxist ideas, it is now found in many circles who have
received it at third or fourth hand and do not know whence it
derives.

The historical fact of the progressive growth of monopoly
during the last fifty years and the increasing restriction of the field
in which competition rules is, of course, not disputed—although
the extent of the phenomenon is often greatly exaggerated.[1] The
important question is whether this development is a necessary
consequence of the advance of technology, or whether it is simply
the result of the policies pursued in most countries. We shall
presently see that the actual history of this development strongly

[1] For a fuller discussion of these problems see Professor L. Robbins's essay
on "The Inevitability of Monopoly" in *The Economic Basis of Class Conflict*,
1939, pp. 45–80.

suggests the latter. But we must first consider in how far modern technological developments are of such a kind as to make the growth of monopolies in wide fields inevitable.

The alleged technological cause of the growth of monopoly is the superiority of the large firm over the small, due to the greater efficiency of modern methods of mass production. Modern methods, it is asserted, have created conditions in the majority of industries where the production of the large firm can be increased at decreasing costs per unit, with the result that the large firms are everywhere underbidding and driving out the small ones ; this process must go on till in each industry only one or at most a few giant firms are left. This argument singles out one effect sometimes accompanying technological progress ; it disregards others which work in the opposite direction ; and it receives little support from a serious study of the facts. We cannot here investigate this question in detail and must be content to accept the best evidence available. The most comprehensive study of the facts undertaken in recent times is that of the American " Temporary National Economic Committee " on the *Concentration of Economic Power*. The final report of this Committee (which certainly cannot be accused of an undue liberal bias) arrives at the conclusion that the view according to which the greater efficiency of large-scale production is the cause of the disappearance of competition " finds scant support in any evidence that is now at hand ".[1] And the detailed monograph on the question which was prepared for the Committee sums up the answer in this statement :

> The superior efficiency of large establishments has not been demonstrated ; the advantages that are supposed to destroy competition have failed to manifest themselves in many fields. Nor do the economies of size, where they exist, invariably necessitate monopoly. . . . The size or the sizes of the optimum efficiency may be reached long before the major part of a supply is subjected to such control. The conclusions that the advantage of large-scale production must lead inevitably to the abolition of competition cannot be accepted. It should be noted, moreover, that monopoly is frequently the product of factors other than the lower costs of greater size. It is attained through collusive agreement and promoted by public policies. When these agreements are invalidated and when these policies are reversed, competitive conditions can be restored.[2]

An investigation of conditions in this country would lead to very similar results. Anyone who has observed how aspiring

---

[1] *Final Report and Recommendations of the Temporary National Economic Committee*, 77th Congress, 1st Session, Senate Document No. 35, 1941, p. 89.
[2] C. Wilcox, *Competition and Monopoly in American Industry*, Temporary National Economic Committee, Monograph No. 21, 1940, p. 314.

monopolists regularly seek and frequently obtain the assistance
of the power of the state to make their control effective can have
little doubt that there is nothing inevitable about this development.

*   *   *   *   *

This conclusion is strongly supported by the historical order
in which the decline of competition and the growth of monopoly
manifested themselves in different countries.   If they were the
result of technological developments or a necessary product of
the evolution of " capitalism ", we should expect them to appear
first in the countries with the most advanced economic system.
In fact they appeared first during the last third of the nineteenth
century in what were then comparatively young industrial
countries, the United States and Germany.   In the latter country
especially, which came to be regarded as the model country
typifying the necessary evolution of capitalism, the growth
of cartels and syndicates has since 1878 been systematically
fostered by deliberate policy.   Not only the instrument of protection, but direct inducements and ultimately compulsion, were
used by the governments to further the creation of monopolies
for the regulation of prices and sales.   It was here that, with the
help of the state, the first great experiment in " scientific planning "
and " conscious organisation of industry " led to the creation of
giant monopolies, which were represented as inevitable growths
fifty years before the same was done in Great Britain.   It is
largely due to the influence of German socialist theoreticians,
particularly Sombart, generalising from the experience of their
country, that the inevitable development of the competitive
system into " monopoly capitalism " became widely accepted.
That in the United States a highly protectionist policy made
a somewhat similar development possible, seemed to confirm
this generalisation.   The development of Germany, however,
more than that of the United States, came to be regarded as
representative of a universal tendency ; and it became a commonplace to speak—to quote a widely read political essay of recent
date—of " Germany where all the social and political forces of
modern civilisation have reached their most advanced form ".[1]
How little there was of inevitability in all this, and how much
is the result of deliberate policy, becomes clear when we consider
the position in this country till 1931 and the development since
that year in which Great Britain also embarked upon a policy of
general protection.   It is only a dozen years since, except for a
few industries which had obtained protection earlier, British
industry was on the whole as competitive as, perhaps, at any time
in its history.   And, although during the 1920's it suffered

[1] R. Niebuhr, *Moral Man and Immoral Society*, 1932.

severely from incompatible policies followed with regard to wages
and to money, at least the years till 1929 compare with regard to
employment and general activity not unfavourably with the 1930's.
It is only since the transition to protection and the general change
in British economic policy accompanying it, that the growth
of monopolies has proceeded at an amazing rate and has transformed British industry to an extent the public has scarcely yet
realised.   To argue that this development has anything to do
with the technological progress during this period, that technological necessities which in Germany operated in the 1880's and
1890's, made themselves felt here in the 1930's, is not much less
absurd than the claim, implied in the statement of Mussolini
(quoted at the head of this chapter) that Italy had to abolish
individual freedom before other European people because its
civilisation had marched so far in advance of the rest !

In so far as this country is concerned, the thesis that the change
in opinion and policy merely follows an inexorable change in the
facts can be given a certain appearance of truth, just because
England has followed at a distance the intellectual developments
elsewhere.   It could thus be argued that monopolistic organisation
of industry grew up in spite of the fact that public opinion still
favoured competition, but that outside events frustrated their
wishes.   The true relation between theory and practice becomes,
however, clear as soon as we look to the prototype of this development, Germany.   That *there* the suppression of competition was
a matter of deliberate policy, that it was undertaken in the service
of the ideal which we now call planning, there can be no doubt.
In the progressive advance towards a completely planned society
the Germans, and all the people who are imitating their example,
are merely following the course which nineteenth-century thinkers,
particularly Germans, have mapped out for them.   The intellectual history of the last sixty or eighty years is indeed a perfect
illustration of the truth that in social evolution nothing is inevitable
but thinking makes it so.

*   *   *   *   *

The assertion that modern technological progress makes
planning inevitable can also be interpreted in a different manner.
It may mean that the complexity of our modern industrial
civilisation creates new problems with which we cannot hope to
deal effectively except by central planning.   In a sense this is
true—yet not in the wide sense in which it is claimed.   It is, for
example, a commonplace that many of the problems created by
a modern town, like many other problems caused by close
contiguity in space, are not adequately solved by competition.
But it is not these problems, like those of the " public utilities ",

etc., which are uppermost in the minds of those who invoke the complexity of modern civilisation as an argument for central planning. What they generally suggest is that the increasing difficulty of obtaining a coherent picture of the complete economic process makes it indispensable that things should be co-ordinated by some central agency if social life is not to dissolve in chaos.

This argument is based on a complete misapprehension of the working of competition. Far from being appropriate only to comparatively simple conditions, it is the very complexity of the division of labour under modern conditions which makes competition the only method by which such co-ordination can be adequately brought about. There would be no difficulty about efficient control or planning were conditions so simple that a single person or board could effectively survey all the relevant facts. It is only as the factors which have to be taken into account become so numerous that it is impossible to gain a synoptic view of them, that decentralisation becomes imperative. But once decentralisation is necessary, the problem of co-ordination arises, a co-ordination which leaves the separate agencies free to adjust their activities to the facts which only they can know, and yet brings about a mutual adjustment of their respective plans. As decentralisation has become necessary because nobody can consciously balance all the considerations bearing on the decisions of so many individuals, the co-ordination can clearly not be effected by " conscious control ", but only by arrangements which convey to each agent the information he must possess in order effectively to adjust his decisions to those of others. And because all the details of the changes constantly affecting the conditions of demand and supply of the different commodities can never be fully known, or quickly enough be collected and disseminated, by any one centre, what is required is some apparatus of registration which automatically records all the relevant effects of individual actions, and whose indications are at the same time the resultant of, and the guide for, all the individual decisions.

This is precisely what the price system does under competition, and which no other system even promises to accomplish. It enables entrepreneurs, by watching the movement of comparatively few prices, as an engineer watches the hands of a few dials, to adjust their activities to those of their fellows. The important point here is that the price system will fulfil this function only if competition prevails, that is, if the individual producer has to adapt himself to price changes and cannot control them. The more complicated the whole, the more dependent we become on that division of knowledge between individuals whose separate efforts are co-ordinated by the impersonal mechanism for transmitting the relevant information known by us as the price system.

It is no exaggeration to say that if we had had to rely on conscious central planning for the growth of our industrial system, it would never have reached the degree of differentiation, complexity, and flexibility it has attained. Compared with this method of solving the economic problem by means of decentralisation plus automatic co-ordination, the more obvious method of central direction is incredibly clumsy, primitive, and limited in scope. That the division of labour has reached the extent which makes modern civilisation possible we owe to the fact that it did not have to be consciously created, but that man tumbled on a method by which the division of labour could be extended far beyond the limits within which it could have been planned. Any further growth of its complexity, therefore, far from making central direction more necessary, makes it more important than ever that we should use a technique which does not depend on conscious control.

*   *   *   *   *

There is yet another theory which connects the growth of monopolies with technological progress, and which uses arguments almost opposite to those we have just considered ; though not often clearly stated, it has also exercised considerable influence. It contends, not that modern technique destroys competition, but that, on the contrary, it will be impossible to make use of many of the new technological possibilities unless protection against competition is granted, i.e., a monopoly is conferred. This type of argument is not necessarily fraudulent, as the critical reader will perhaps suspect : the obvious answer, that if a new technique for satisfying our wants is really better, it ought to be able to stand up against all competition, does not dispose of all instances to which this argument refers. No doubt in many cases it is used merely as a form of special pleading by interested parties. Even more often it is probably based on a confusion between technical excellence from a narrow engineering point of view and desirability from the point of view of society as a whole.

There remains, however, a group of instances where the argument has some force. It is, for example, at least conceivable that the British automobile industry might be able to supply a car cheaper and better than cars used to be in the United States if everyone in this country were made to use the same kind of car ; or that the use of electricity for all purposes could be made cheaper than coal or gas if everybody could be made to use only electricity. In instances like these it is at least possible that we might all be better off, and should prefer the new situation if we had the choice —but that no individual ever gets the choice, because the alternative is that either we should all use the same cheap car (or all should use only electricity), or that we should have the choice between these things with each of them at a much higher price. I do not know whether this is true in either of the instances given. But it must be admitted that it is possible that by compulsory standardisation or the prohibition of variety beyond a certain degree, abundance might be increased in some fields more than sufficiently to compensate for the restriction of the choice of the consumer. It is even conceivable that a new invention may be made some day whose adoption would seem unquestionably beneficial, but which could be used only if many or all people were made to avail themselves of it at the same time.

Whether such instances are of any great or lasting importance, they are certainly not instances where it could be legitimately claimed that technical progress makes central direction inevitable. They would merely make it necessary to choose between gaining a particular advantage by compulsion and not obtaining it—or, in most instances, obtaining it a little later, when further technical advance has overcome the particular difficulties. It is true that in such situations we may have to sacrifice a possible immediate gain as the price of our freedom—but we avoid, on the other hand, the necessity of making future developments dependent upon the knowledge which particular people now possess. By sacrificing such possible present advantages we preserve an important stimulus to further progress. Though in the short run the price we have to pay for variety and freedom of choice may sometimes be high, in the long run even material progress will depend on this very variety, because we can never predict from which of the many forms in which a good or service can be provided something better may develop. It cannot, of course, be asserted that the preservation of freedom at the expense of some addition to our present material comfort will be thus rewarded in all instances. But the argument for freedom is precisely that we ought to leave room for the unforeseeable free growth. It applies, therefore, no less when, on the basis of our present knowledge, compulsion would seem to bring only advantages, and although in a particular instance it may actually do no harm.

In much of the current discussion on the effects of technological progress this progress is presented to us as if it were something outside us which could compel us to use the new knowledge in a particular way. While it is true, of course, that inventions have given us tremendous power, it is absurd to suggest that we must use this power to destroy our most precious inheritance : liberty. It does mean, however, that if we want to preserve it, we must guard it more jealously than ever and that we must be prepared to make sacrifices for it. While there is nothing in modern technological developments which forces us towards comprehensive economic planning, there is a great deal in them which makes infinitely more dangerous the power a planning-authority would possess.

* * * * *

While there can thus be little doubt that the movement towards planning is the result of deliberate action and that there are no external necessities which force us to it, it is worth enquiring why so large a proportion of the technical experts should be found in the front rank of the planners. The explanation of this pheno-menon is closely connected with an important fact which the critics of the planners should always keep in mind : that there is little question that almost every one of the technical ideals of our experts could be realised within a comparatively short time if to achieve them were made the sole aim of humanity. There is an infinite number of good things, which we all agree are highly desirable as well as possible, but of which we cannot hope to achieve more than a few within our lifetime, or which we can hope to achieve only very imperfectly. It is the frustration of his ambitions in his own field which makes the specialist revolt against the existing order. We all find it difficult to bear to see things left undone which everybody must admit are both desir-able and possible. That these things cannot all be done at the same time, that any one of them can be achieved only at the sacrifice of others, can be seen only by taking into account factors which fall outside any specialism, which can be appreciated only by a painful intellectual effort—the more painful as it forces us to see against a wider background the objects to which most of our labours are directed, and to balance them against others which lie outside our immediate interest and for which, for that reason, we care less.

Every one of the many things which, considered in isolation, it would be possible to achieve in a planned society, creates enthu-siasts for planning who feel confident that they will be able to instil into the directors of such a society their sense of the value of the particular objective ; and the hopes of some of them would undoubtedly be fulfilled, since a planned society would certainly further some objectives more than is the case at present. It would be foolish to deny that the instances of planned or semi-planned societies which we know do furnish illustrations in point, good things which the people of these countries owe entirely to planning. The magnificent motor roads in Germany and Italy are an instance often quoted—even though they do not represent a kind of planning not equally possible in a liberal society. But it is equally foolish to quote such instances of technical excellence in particular fields as evidence of the general superiority of planning. It would be more correct to say that such extreme technical excellence out of line with general conditions is evidence of a misdirection of resources. Anyone who has driven along the famous German motor roads and found the amount of traffic on them less than on many a secondary road in England, can have little doubt that, so far as peace purposes are concerned, there was little justification for them. Whether it was not a case where the planners decided in favour of " guns " instead of " butter " is another matter.[1] But by our standards there is little ground for enthusiasm.

The illusion of the specialist that in a planned society he would secure more attention to the objectives for which he cares most is a more general phenomenon than the term of specialist at first suggests. In our predilections and interests we are all in some measure specialists. And we all think that our personal order of values is not merely personal, but that in a free discussion among rational people we would convince the others that ours is the right one. The lover of the country-side who wants above all that its traditional appearance should be preserved and that the blots already made by industry on its fair face should be removed, no less than the health enthusiast who wants all the picturesque but insanitary old cottages cleared away, or the motorist who wishes the country cut up by big motor roads, the efficiency fanatic who desires the maximum of specialisation and mechanisation no less than the idealist who for the development of personality wants to preserve as many independent craftsmen as possible, all know that their aim can be fully achieved only by planning—and they all want planning for that reason. But, of course, the adoption of the social planning for which they clamour can only bring out the concealed conflict between their aims.

The movement for planning owes its present strength largely to the fact that, while planning is in the main still an ambition, it unites almost all the single-minded idealists, all the men and women who have devoted their lives to a single task. The hopes they place in planning, however, are not the result of a comprehensive view of society, but rather of a very limited view, and often the result of a great exaggeration of the importance of the ends they place foremost. This is not to underrate the great pragmatic value of this type of men in a free society like ours, which makes them the subject of just admiration. But it would make the very men who are most anxious to plan society the most dangerous if they were allowed to do so—and the most intolerant of the planning of others. From the saintly and single-

[1] But as I am correcting this the news comes that maintenance work on the German motor roads has been suspended !

minded idealist to the fanatic is often but a step. Though it is the resentment of the frustrated specialist which gives the demand for planning its strongest impetus, there could hardly be a more unbearable—and more irrational—world than one in which the most eminent specialists in each field were allowed to proceed unchecked with the realisation of their ideals. Nor can " co-ordination ", as some planners seem to imagine, become a new specialism. The economist is the last to claim that he has the knowledge which the co-ordinator would need. His plea is for a method which effects such co-ordination without the need for an omniscient dictator. But that means precisely the retention of some such impersonal and often unintelligible checks on individual efforts as those against which all specialists chafe.

CHAPTER V

PLANNING AND DEMOCRACY

> The statesman who should attempt to direct private people in what manner they ought to employ their capitals, would not only load himself with a most unnecessary attention, but assume an authority which could safely be trusted to no council and senate whatever, and which would nowhere be so dangerous as in the hands of a man who had folly and presumption enough to fancy himself fit to exercise it.
>
> *Adam Smith.*

THE common features of all collectivist systems may be described, in a phrase ever dear to socialists of all schools, as the deliberate organisation of the labours of society for a definite social goal. That our present society lacks such " conscious " direction towards a single aim, that its activities are guided by the whims and fancies of irresponsible individuals, has always been one of the main complaints of its socialist critics.

In many ways this puts the basic issue very clearly. And it directs us at once to the point where the conflict arises between individual freedom and collectivism. The various kinds of collectivism, communism, fascism, etc., differ between themselves in the nature of the goal towards which they want to direct the efforts of society. But they all differ from liberalism and individualism in wanting to organise the whole of society and all its resources for this unitary end, and in refusing to recognise autonomous spheres in which the ends of the individuals are supreme. In short, they are totalitarian in the true sense of this new word which we have adopted to describe the unexpected but nevertheless inseparable manifestations of what in theory we call collectivism.

The " social goal ", or " common purpose ", for which society is to be organised, is usually vaguely described as the " common good ", or the " general welfare ", or the " general interest ". It does not need much reflection to see that these terms have no sufficiently definite meaning to determine a particular course of action. The welfare and the happiness of millions cannot be measured on a single scale of less and more. The welfare of a people, like the happiness of a man, depends on a great many things that can be provided in an infinite variety of combinations. It cannot be adequately expressed as a single end, but only as a hierarchy of ends, a comprehensive scale of values in which every need of every person is given its place. To direct all our activities according to a single plan presupposes that

42

every one of our needs is given its rank in an order of values which must be complete enough to make it possible to decide between all the different courses between which the planner has to choose. It presupposes, in short, the existence of a complete ethical code in which all the different human values are allotted their due place.

The conception of a complete ethical code is unfamiliar and it requires some effort of imagination to see what it involves. We are not in the habit of thinking of moral codes as more or less complete. The fact that we are constantly choosing between different values without a social code prescribing how we ought to choose, does not surprise us, and does not suggest to us that our moral code is incomplete. In our society there is neither occasion nor reason why people should develop common views about what should be done in such situations. But where all the means to be used are the property of society, and are to be used in the name of society according to a unitary plan, a " social " view about what ought to be done must guide all decisions. In such a world we should soon find that our moral code is full of gaps.

We are not concerned here with the question whether it would be desirable to have such a complete ethical code. It may merely be pointed out that up to the present the growth of civilisation has been accompanied by a steady diminution of the sphere in which individual actions are bound by fixed rules. The rules of which our common moral code consists have progressively become fewer and more general in character. From the primitive man who was bound by an elaborate ritual in almost every one of his daily activities, who was limited by innumerable taboos, and who could scarcely conceive of doing things in a way different from his fellows, morals have more and more tended to become merely limits circumscribing the sphere within which the individual could behave as he liked. The adoption of a common ethical code comprehensive enough to determine a unitary economic plan would mean a complete reversal of this tendency.

The essential point for us is that no such complete ethical code exists. The attempt to direct all economic activity according to a single plan would raise innumerable questions to which the answer could be provided only by a moral rule, but to which existing morals have no answer and where there exists no agreed view on what ought to be done. People will have either no definite views or conflicting views on such questions, because in the free society in which we have lived there has been no occasion to think about them and still less to form common opinions about them.

* * * * *

Not only do we not possess such an all-inclusive scale of values : it would be impossible for any mind to comprehend the infinite variety of different needs of different people which compete for the available resources and to attach a definite weight to each. For our problem it is of minor importance whether the ends for which any person cares comprehend only his own individual needs, or whether they include the needs of his closer or even those of his more distant fellows—that is, whether he is egoistic or altruistic in the ordinary senses of these words. The point which is so important is the basic fact that it is impossible for any man to survey more than a limited field, to be aware of the urgency of more than a limited number of needs. Whether his interests centre round his own physical needs, or whether he takes a warm interest in the welfare of every human being he knows, the ends about which he can be concerned will always be only an infinitesimal fraction of the needs of all men.

This is the fundamental fact on which the whole philosophy of individualism is based. It does not assume, as is often asserted, that man is egoistic or selfish, or ought to be. It merely starts from the indisputable fact that the limits of our powers of imagination make it impossible to include in our scale of values more than a sector of the needs of the whole society, and that, since, strictly speaking, scales of value can exist only in individual minds, nothing but partial scales of values exist, scales which are inevitably different and often inconsistent with each other. From this the individualist concludes that the individuals should be allowed, within defined limits, to follow their own values and preferences rather than somebody else's, that within these spheres the individual's system of ends should be supreme and not subject to any dictation by others. It is this recognition of the individual as the ultimate judge of his ends, the belief that as far as possible his own views ought to govern his actions, that forms the essence of the individualist position.

This view does not, of course, exclude the recognition of social ends, or rather of a coincidence of individual ends which makes it advisable for men to combine for their pursuit. But it limits such common action to the instances where individual views coincide ; what are called " social ends " are for it merely identical ends of many individuals—or ends to the achievement of which individuals are willing to contribute in return for the assistance they receive in the satisfaction of their own desires. Common action is thus limited to the fields where people agree on common ends. Very frequently these common ends will not be ultimate ends to the individuals, but means which different persons can use for different purposes. In fact, people are most likely to agree on common action where the common end is not an ultimate end to them, but a means capable of serving a great variety of purposes.

When individuals combine in a joint effort to realise ends they have in common, the organisations, like the state, that they form for this purpose, are given their own system of ends and their own means. But any organisation thus formed remains one " person " among others, in the case of the state much more powerful than any of the others, it is true, yet still with its separate and limited sphere in which alone its ends are supreme. The limits of this sphere are determined by the extent to which the individuals agree on particular ends ; and the probability that they will agree on a particular course of action necessarily decreases as the scope of such action extends. There are certain functions of the state on the exercise of which there will be practical unanimity among its citizens ; there will be others on which there will be agreement of a substantial majority ; and so on, till we come to fields where, although each individual might wish the state to act in some way, there will be almost as many views about what the government should do as there are different people.

We can rely on voluntary agreement to guide the action of the state only so long as it is confined to spheres where agreement exists. But not only when the state undertakes direct control in fields where there is no such agreement is it bound to suppress individual freedom. We can unfortunately not indefinitely extend the sphere of common action and still leave the individual free in his own sphere. Once the communal sector, in which the state controls all the means, exceeds a certain proportion of the whole, the effects of its actions dominate the whole system. Although the state controls directly the use of only a large part of the available resources, the effects of its decisions on the remaining part of the economic system become so great that indirectly it controls almost everything. Where, as was, for example, true in Germany as early as 1928, the central and local authorities directly control the use of more than half the national income (according to an official German estimate then, 53 per cent.) they control indirectly almost the whole economic life of the nation. There is, then, scarcely an individual end which is not dependent for its achievement on the action of the state, and the " social scale of values " which guides the state's action must embrace practically all individual ends.

* * * * *

It is not difficult to see what must be the consequences when democracy embarks upon a course of planning which in its execution requires more agreement than in fact exists. The people may have agreed on adopting a system of directed economy because they have been convinced that it will produce great prosperity. In the discussions leading to the decision, the goal of planning will have been described by some such term as " common welfare " which only conceals the absence of real agreement on the ends of planning. Agreement will in fact exist only on the mechanism to be used. But it is a mechanism which can be used only for a common end ; and the question of the precise goal towards which all activity is to be directed will arise as soon as the executive power has to translate the demand for a single plan into a particular plan. Then it will appear that the agreement on the desirability of planning is not supported by agreement on the ends the plan is to serve. The effect of the people agreeing that there must be central planning, without agreeing on the ends, will be rather as if a group of people were to commit themselves to take a journey together without agreeing where they want to go : with the result that they may all have to make a journey which most of them do not want at all. That planning creates a situation in which it is necessary for us to agree on a much larger number of topics than we have been used to, and that in a planned system we cannot confine collective action to the tasks on which we can agree, but are forced to produce agreement on everything in order that any action can be taken at all, is one of the features which contribute more than most to determining the character of a planned system.

It may have been the unanimously expressed will of the people that parliament should prepare a comprehensive economic plan, yet neither the people nor its representatives need therefore be able to agree on any particular plan. The inability of demo-cratic assemblies to carry out what seems to be a clear mandate of the people will inevitably cause dissatisfaction with democratic institutions. Parliaments come to be regarded as ineffective " talking shops ", unable or incompetent to carry out the tasks for which they have been chosen. The conviction grows that if efficient planning is to be done, the direction must be " taken out of politics " and placed in the hands of experts, permanent officials or independent autonomous bodies.

The difficulty is well known to socialists. It will soon be half a century since the Webbs began to complain of " the increased incapacity of the House of Commons to cope with its work ".[1] More recently, Professor Laski has elaborated the argument :

> It is common ground that the present parliamentary machine is quite unsuited to pass rapidly a great body of complicated legislation.

---

[1] S. and B. Webb, *Industrial Democracy*, 1897, p. 800, footnote.

The National Government, indeed, has in substance admitted this by implementing its economy and tariff measures not by detailed debate in the House of Commons but by a wholesale system of delegated legislation. A Labour Government would, I presume, build upon the amplitude of this precedent. It would confine the House of Commons to the two functions it can properly perform : the ventilation of grievances and the discussion of general principles of its measures. Its Bills would take the form of general formulæ conferring wide powers on the appropriate government departments ; and those powers would be exercised by Order in Council which could, if desired, be attacked in the House by means of a vote of no confidence. The necessity and value of delegated legislation has recently been strongly reaffirmed by the Donoughmore Committee ; and its extension is inevitable if the process of socialisation is not to be wrecked by the normal methods of obstruction which existing parliamentary procedure sanctions.

And to make it quite clear that a socialist government must not allow itself to be too much fettered by democratic procedure, Professor Laski at the end of the same article raised the question " whether in a period of transition to Socialism, a Labour Government can risk the overthrow of its measures as a result of the next general election "—and left it significantly unanswered.[1]

*   *   *   *   *

It is important clearly to see the causes of this admitted ineffectiveness of parliaments when it comes to a detailed administration of the economic affairs of a nation. The fault is neither with the individual representatives nor with parliamentary institutions as such, but with the contradictions inherent in the task with which they are charged. They are not asked to act where they can agree, but to produce agreement on everything—the whole direction of the resources of the nation. For such a task the system of majority decision is, however, not suited. Majorities will be found where it is a choice between limited alternatives ; but it is a superstition to believe that there must be a majority view on everything. There is no reason why there should be

[1] H. J. Laski, " Labour and the Constitution ", *The New Statesman and Nation*, No. 81 (New Series), Sept. 10th, 1932, p. 277. In a book (*Democracy in Crisis*, 1933, particularly p. 87) in which Professor Laski later elaborated these ideas, his determination that parliamentary democracy must not be allowed to form an obstacle to the realisation of socialism is even more plainly expressed : not only would a socialist government " take vast powers and legislate under them by ordinance and decree " and " suspend the classic formulæ of normal opposition ", but the " continuance of parliamentary government would depend on its [i.e. the Labour Government's] possession of guarantees from the Conservative Party that its work of transformation would not be disrupted by repeal in the event of its defeat at the polls " !
As Professor Laski invokes the authority of the Donoughmore Committee it may be worth recalling that Professor Laski was a member of that committee and presumably one of the authors of its report.

a majority in favour of any one of the different possible courses of positive action if their number is legion. Every member of the legislative assembly might prefer some particular plan for the direction of economic activity to no plan, yet no one plan may appear preferable to a majority to no plan at all.

Nor can a coherent plan be achieved by breaking it up into parts and voting on particular issues. A democratic assembly voting and amending a comprehensive economic plan clause by clause, as it deliberates on an ordinary bill, makes nonsense. An economic plan, to deserve the name, must have a unitary conception. Even if parliament could, proceeding step by step, agree on some scheme, it would certainly in the end satisfy nobody. A complex whole where all the parts must be most carefully adjusted to each other, cannot be achieved through a compromise between conflicting views. To draw up an economic plan in this fashion is even less possible than, for example, successfully to plan a military campaign by democratic procedure. As in strategy it would become inevitable to delegate the task to the experts.

Yet the difference is that, while the general who is put in charge of a campaign is given a single end to which, for the duration of the campaign, all the means under his control have to be exclusively devoted, there can be no such single goal given to the economic planner, and no similar limitation of the means imposed upon him. The general has not got to balance different independent aims against each other ; there is for him only one supreme goal. But the ends of an economic plan, or of any part of it, cannot be defined apart from the particular plan. It is the essence of the economic problem that the making of an economic plan involves the choice between conflicting or competing ends—different needs of different people. But which ends do so conflict, which will have to be sacrificed if we want to achieve certain others, in short, which are the alternatives between which we must choose, can only be known to those who know all the facts ; and only they, the experts, are in a position to decide which of the different ends are to be given preference. It is inevitable that they should impose their scale of preferences on the community for which they plan.

This is not always clearly recognised and delegation is usually justified by the technical character of the task. But this does not mean that only the technical detail is delegated, or even that the inability of parliaments to understand the technical detail is the root of the difficulty.[1] Alterations in the structure

---

[1] It is instructive in this connection briefly to refer to the Government document in which in recent years these problems have been discussed. As long as thirteen years ago, that is before this country finally abandoned economic liberalism, the process of delegating legislative powers had already been carried

of civil law are no less technical and no more difficult to appreciate in all their implications ; yet nobody has yet seriously suggested that legislation there should be delegated to a body of experts. The fact is that in these fields legislation does not go beyond general rules on which true majority agreement can be achieved, while in the direction of economic activity the interests to be reconciled are so divergent that no true agreement is likely to be reached in a democratic assembly.

It should be recognised, however, that it is not the delegation of law-making power as such, which is so objectionable. To oppose delegation as such is to oppose a symptom instead of the cause and, as it may be a necessary result of other causes, to weaken the case. So long as the power that is delegated is merely the power to make general rules, there may be very good reasons why such rules should be laid down by local rather than by the central authority. The objectionable feature is that delegation is so often resorted to because the matter in hand cannot be regulated by general rules but only by the exercise of discretion in the decision of particular cases. In these instances delegation means that some authority is given power to make with the force of law what to all intents and purposes are arbitrary decisions (usually described as " judging the case on its merits ").

The delegation of particular technical tasks to separate bodies, while a regular feature, is yet only the first step in the process whereby a democracy which embarks on planning progressively relinquishes its powers. The expedient of delegation cannot really remove the causes which make all the advocates of comprehensive planning so impatient with the impotence of democracy. The delegation of particular powers to separate agencies creates

---

to a point where it was felt necessary to appoint a committee to investigate " what safeguards are desirable or necessary to secure the sovereignty of Law ". In its report the " Donoughmore Committee " (*Report of the* [Lord Chancellor's] *Committee on Ministers' Powers,* Cmd. 4060, 1932) showed that even at that date Parliament had resorted " to the practice of wholesale and indiscriminate delegation " but regarded this (it was before we had really glanced into the totalitarian abyss !) as an inevitably and relatively innocuous development. And it is probably true that delegation as such need not be a danger to freedom. The interesting point is why delegation had become necessary on such a scale. First place among the causes enumerated in the report is given to the fact that " Parliament nowadays passes so many laws every year " and that " much of the detail is so technical as to be unsuitable for Parliamentary discussion ". But if this were all there would be no reason why the detail should not be worked out *before* rather than after Parliament passes a law. What is probably in many cases a much more important reason why, " if Parliament were not willing to delegate law-making power, Parliament would be unable to pass the kind and quantity of legislation which public opinion requires " is innocently revealed in the little sentence that " many of the laws affect people's lives so closely that elasticity is essential " ! What does this mean if not conferment of arbitrary power, power limited by no fixed principles and which in the opinion of Parliament cannot be limited by definite and unambiguous rules ?

a new obstacle to the achievement of a single co-ordinated plan.
Even if, by this expedient, a democracy should succeed in planning every sector of economic activity, it would still have to face
the problem of integrating these separate plans into a unitary
whole.   Many separate plans do not make a planned whole—in
fact, as the planners ought to be the first to admit—they may be
worse than no plan.   But the democratic legislature will long
hesitate to relinquish the decisions on really vital issues, and so
long as it does so it makes it impossible for anyone else to provide
the comprehensive plan.   Yet agreement that planning is necessary, together with the inability of democratic assemblies to
produce a plan, will evoke stronger and stronger demands that
the government or some single individual should be given powers
to act on their own responsibility.   The belief is becoming more
and more widespread that, if things are to get done, the responsible
authorities must be freed from the fetters of democratic procedure.

The cry for an economic dictator is a characteristic stage in
the movement towards planning, not unfamiliar in this country.
It is now several years since one of the most acute of foreign
students of England, the late Elie Halévy, suggested that " if
you take a composite photograph of Lord Eustace Percy, Sir
Oswald Mosley, and Sir Stafford Cripps, I think you would
find this common feature—you would find them all agreeing to
say : ' We are living in economic chaos and we cannot get out
of it except under some kind of dictatorial leadership '." [1]   The
number of influential public men whose inclusion would not
materially alter the features of the " composite photograph "
has since grown considerably.

In Germany, even before Hitler came into power, the movement had already progressed much further.   It is important to
remember that for some time before 1933 Germany had reached a
stage in which it had, in effect, had to be governed dictatorially.
Nobody could then doubt that for the time being democracy
had broken down, and that sincere democrats like Brüning were
no more able to govern democratically than Schleicher or von
Papen.   Hitler did not have to destroy democracy ; he merely
took advantage of the decay of democracy and at the critical
moment obtained the support of many to whom, though they
detested Hitler, he yet seemed the only man strong enough to
get things done.

*   *   *   *   *

The argument by which the planners usually try to reconcile
us with this development is that so long as democracy retains

[1] " Socialism and the Problems of Democratic Parliamentarism ", *International Affairs*, vol. XIII, p. 501.

ultimate control, the essentials of democracy are not affected. Thus Karl Mannheim writes :

The only [*sic*] way in which a planned society differs from that of the nineteenth century is that more and more spheres of social life, and ultimately each and all of them, are subjected to state control. But if a few controls can be held in check by parliamentary sovereignty, so can many. . . . in a democratic state sovereignty can be boundlessly strengthened by plenary powers without renouncing democratic control.[1]

This belief overlooks a vital distinction. Parliament can, of course, control the execution of tasks where it can give definite directions, where it has first agreed on the aim and merely delegates the working out of the detail. The situation is entirely different when the reason for the delegation is that there is no real agreement on the ends, when the body charged with the planning has to choose between ends of whose conflict parliament is not even aware, and when the most that can be done is to present to it a plan which has to be accepted or rejected as a whole. There may and probably will be criticism ; but as no majority can agree on an alternative plan, and the parts objected to can almost always be represented as essential parts of the whole, it will remain quite ineffective. Parliamentary discussion may be retained as a useful safety-valve, and even more as a convenient medium through which the official answers to complaints are disseminated. It may even prevent some flagrant abuses and successfully insist on particular shortcomings being remedied. But it cannot direct. It will at best be reduced to choosing the persons who are to have practically absolute power. The whole system will tend towards that plebiscitarian dictatorship in which the head of the government is from time to time confirmed in his position by popular vote, but where he has all the powers at his command to make certain that the vote will go in the direction he desires.

It is the price of democracy that the possibilities of conscious control are restricted to the fields where true agreement exists, and that in some fields things must be left to chance. But in a society which for its functioning depends on central planning, this control cannot be made dependent on a majority being able to agree ; it will often be necessary that the will of a small minority be imposed upon the people, because this minority will be the largest group able to agree among themselves on the question at issue. Democratic government has worked successfully where, and so long as, the functions of government were, by a widely accepted creed, restricted to fields where agreement among a

[1] K. Mannheim, *Man and Society in an Age of Reconstruction*, 1940, p. 340.

majority could be achieved by free discussion ; and it is the great merit of the liberal creed that it reduced the range of subjects on which agreement was necessary to one on which it was likely to exist in a society of free men. It is now often said that democracy will not tolerate " capitalism ". If " capitalism " means here a competitive system based on free disposal over private property, it is far more important to realise that only within this system is democracy possible. When it becomes dominated by a collectivist creed, democracy will inevitably destroy itself.

*   *   *   *   *

We have no intention, however, of making a fetish of democracy. It may well be true that our generation talks and thinks too much of democracy and too little of the values which it serves. It cannot be said of democracy, as Lord Acton truly said of liberty, that it " is not a means to a higher political end. It is itself the highest political end. It is not for the sake of a good public administration that it is required, but for the security in the pursuit of the highest objects of civil society, and of private life." Democracy is essentially a means, a utilitarian device for safeguarding internal peace and individual freedom. As such it is by no means infallible or certain. Nor must we forget that there has often been much more cultural and spiritual freedom under an autocratic rule than under some democracies—and it is at least conceivable that under the government of a very homogeneous and doctrinaire majority democratic government might be as oppressive as the worst dictatorship. Our point, however, is not that dictatorship must inevitably extirpate freedom, but rather that planning leads to dictatorship because dictatorship is the most effective instrument of coercion and the enforcement of ideals, and as such essential if central planning on a large scale is to be possible. The clash between planning and democracy arises simply from the fact that the latter is an obstacle to the suppression of freedom which the direction of economic activity requires. But in so far as democracy ceases to be a guarantee of individual freedom, it may well persist in some form under a totalitarian regime. A true " dictatorship of the proletariat ", even if democratic in form, if it undertook centrally to direct the economic system, would probably destroy personal freedom as completely as any autocracy has ever done.

The fashionable concentration on democracy as the main value threatened is not without danger. It is largely responsible for the misleading and unfounded belief that so long as the ultimate source of power is the will of the majority, the power cannot be arbitrary. The false assurance which many people derive from this belief is an important cause of the general unawareness of the dangers which we face.   There is no justification for the belief that so long as power is conferred by democratic procedure, it cannot be arbitrary ; the contrast suggested by this statement is altogether false : it is not the source but the limitation of power which prevents it from being arbitrary. Democratic control *may* prevent power from becoming arbitrary, but it does not do so by its mere existence.   If democracy resolves on a task which necessarily involves the use of power which cannot be guided by fixed rules, it must become arbitrary power.

CHAPTER VI

PLANNING AND THE RULE OF LAW

> Recent studies in the sociology of law once more confirm
> that the fundamental principle of formal law by which every
> case must be judged according to general rational precepts,
> which have as few exceptions as possible and are based on
> logical subsumptions, obtains only for the liberal competitive
> phase of capitalism.
>
> *K. Mannheim.*

NOTHING distinguishes more clearly conditions in a free
country from those in a country under arbitrary government
than the observance in the former of the great principles known
as the Rule of Law. Stripped of all technicalities this means
that government in all its actions is bound by rules fixed and
announced beforehand—rules which make it possible to foresee
with fair certainty how the authority will use its coercive powers
in given circumstances, and to plan one's individual affairs on
the basis of this knowledge.[1] Though this ideal can never be
perfectly achieved, since legislators as well as those to whom the
administration of the law is entrusted are fallible men, the essential
point, that the discretion left to the executive organs wielding
coercive power should be reduced as much as possible, is clear
enough. While every law restricts individual freedom to some
extent by altering the means which people may use in the pursuit
of their aims, under the Rule of Law the government is prevented from stultifying individual efforts by *ad hoc* action.
Within the known rules of the game the individual is free
to pursue his personal ends and desires, certain that the powers
of government will not be used deliberately to frustrate his
efforts.

The distinction we have drawn before between the creation of
a permanent framework of laws within which the productive
activity is guided by individual decisions, and the direction of

---

[1] According to the classical exposition by A. V. Dicey in *The Law of the
Constitution* (8th ed., p. 198) the rule of law " means, in the first place, the
absolute supremacy or predominance of regular law as opposed to the influence
of arbitrary power, and excludes the existence of arbitrariness, of prerogative,
or even of wide discretionary authority on the part of government ". Largely
as a result of Dicey's work the term has, however, in England acquired a
narrower technical meaning which does not concern us here. The wider and
older meaning of the concept of the rule or reign of law, which in England had
become an established tradition which was more taken for granted than discussed, has been most fully elaborated, just because it raised what were there
new problems, in the early nineteenth-century discussions in Germany about
the nature of the *Rechtsstaat*.

economic activity by a central authority, is thus really a particular case of the more general distinction between the Rule of Law and arbitrary government. Under the first the government confines itself to fixing rules determining the conditions under which the available resources may be used, leaving to the individuals the decision for what ends they are to be used. Under the second the government directs the use of the means of production to particular ends. The first type of rules can be made in advance, in the shape of *formal rules* which do not aim at the wants and needs of particular people. They are intended to be merely instrumental in the pursuit of people's various individual ends. And they are, or ought to be, intended for such long periods that it is impossible to know whether they will assist particular people more than others. They could almost be described as a kind of instrument of production, helping people to predict the behaviour of those with whom they must collaborate, rather than as efforts towards the satisfaction of particular needs.

Economic planning of the collectivist kind necessarily involves the very opposite of this. The planning authority cannot confine itself to providing opportunities for unknown people to make whatever use of them they like. It cannot tie itself down in advance to general and formal rules which prevent arbitrariness. It must provide for the actual needs of people as they arise and then choose deliberately between them. It must constantly decide questions which cannot be answered by formal principles only, and in making these decisions it must set up distinctions of merit between the needs of different people. When the government has to decide how many pigs are to be reared or how many buses are to be run, which coal mines are to operate, or at what prices boots are to be sold, these decisions cannot be deduced from formal principles, or settled for long periods in advance. They depend inevitably on the circumstances of the moment, and in making such decisions it will always be necessary to balance one against the other the interests of various persons and groups. In the end somebody's views will have to decide whose interests are more important; and these views must become part of the law of the land, a new distinction of rank which the coercive apparatus of government imposes upon the people.

* * * * *

The distinction we have just used between formal law or justice and substantive rules is very important and at the same time most difficult to draw precisely in practice. Yet the general principle involved is simple enough. The difference between the two kinds of rules is the same as that between laying down a Rule of the Road, as in the Highway Code, and ordering people where to go; or, better still, between providing signposts and commanding people which road to take. The formal rules tell people in advance what action the state will take in certain types of situation, defined in general terms, without reference to time and place or particular people. They refer to typical situations into which anyone may get and in which the existence of such rules will be useful for a great variety of individual purposes. The knowledge that in such situations the state will act in a definite way, or require people to behave in a certain manner, is provided as a means for people to use in making their own plans. Formal rules are thus merely instrumental in the sense that they are expected to be useful to yet unknown people, for purposes for which these people will decide to use them, and in circumstances which cannot be foreseen in detail. In fact, that we do *not* know their concrete effect, that we do *not* know what particular ends these rules will further, or which particular people they will assist, that they are merely given the form most likely on the whole to benefit all the people affected by them, is the most important criterion of formal rules in the sense in which we here use this term. They do not involve a choice between particular ends or particular people, because we just cannot know beforehand by whom and in what way they will be used.

In our age, with its passion for conscious control of everything, it may appear paradoxical to claim as a virtue that under one system we shall know less about the particular effect of the measures the state takes than would be true under most other systems and that a method of social control should be deemed superior because of our ignorance of its precise results. Yet this consideration is in fact the *rationale* of the great liberal principle of the Rule of Law. And the apparent paradox dissolves rapidly when we follow the argument a little further.

*   *   *   *   *

This argument is two-fold; the first is economic and can here only briefly be stated. The state should confine itself to establishing rules applying to general types of situations, and should allow the individuals freedom in everything which depends on the circumstances of time and place, because only the individuals concerned in each instance can fully know these circumstances and adapt their actions to them. If the individuals are to be able to use their knowledge effectively in making plans, they must be able to predict actions of the state which may affect these plans. But if the actions of the state are to be predictable, they must be determined by rules fixed independently of the concrete circumstances which can neither be foreseen nor taken into account beforehand : and the particular effects of such actions will be unpredictable. If, on the other hand, the state were to direct the individual's actions so as to achieve particular ends, its action would have to be decided on the basis of the full circumstances of the moment and would therefore be unpredictable. Hence the familiar fact that the more the state " plans " the more difficult planning becomes for the individual.

The second, moral or political, argument is even more directly relevant to the point under discussion. If the state is precisely to foresee the incidence of its actions, it means that it can leave those affected no choice. Wherever the state can exactly foresee the effects on particular people of alternative courses of action, it is also the state which chooses between the different ends. If we want to create new opportunities open to all, to offer chances of which people can make what use they like, the precise results cannot be foreseen. General rules, genuine laws as distinguished from specific orders, must therefore be intended to operate in circumstances which cannot be foreseen in detail, and, therefore, their effect on particular ends or particular people cannot be known beforehand. It is in this sense alone that it is at all possible for the legislator to be impartial. To be impartial means to have no answer to certain questions—to the kind of questions which, if we have to decide them, we decide by tossing a coin. In a world where everything was precisely foreseen, the state could hardly do anything and remain impartial. But where the precise effects of government policy on particular people are known, where the government aims directly at such particular effects, it cannot help knowing these effects, and therefore it cannot be impartial. It must, of necessity, take sides, impose its valuations upon people and, instead of assisting them in the advancement of their own ends, choose the ends for them. As soon as the particular effects are foreseen at the time a law is made, it ceases to be a mere instrument to be used by the people and becomes instead an instrument used by the law-giver upon the people and for his ends. The state ceases to be a piece of utilitarian machinery intended to help individuals in the fullest development of their individual personality and becomes a " moral " institution—where " moral " is not used in contrast to immoral, but describes an institution which imposes on its members its views on all moral questions, whether these views be moral or highly immoral. In this sense the Nazi or any other collectivist state is " moral ", while the liberal state is not.

Perhaps it will be said that all this raises no serious problem because in the kind of questions which the economic planner would have to decide he need not and should not be guided by his individual prejudices, but could rely on the general conviction

of what is fair and reasonable.   This contention usually receives
support from those who have experience of planning in a particular
industry and who find that there is no insuperable difficulty about
arriving at a decision which all those immediately interested will
accept as fair.   The reason why this experience proves nothing
is, of course, the selection of the " interests " concerned when
planning is confined to a particular industry.   Those most
immediately interested in a particular issue are not necessarily
the best judges of the interests of society as a whole.   To take
only the most characteristic case : when capital and labour in
an industry agree on some policy of restriction and thus exploit
the consumers, there is usually no difficulty about the division
of the spoils in proportion to former earnings or on some similar
principle.   The loss which is divided between thousands or
millions is usually either simply disregarded or quite inadequately
considered.   If we want to test the usefulness of the principle
of " fairness " in deciding the kind of issues which arise in
economic planning, we must apply it to some question where
the gains and the losses are seen equally clearly.   In such instances
it is readily recognised that no general principle such as fairness
can provide an answer.   When we have to choose between
higher wages for nurses or doctors and more extensive services
for the sick, more milk for children and better wages for agri-
cultural workers, or between employment for the unemployed
or better wages for those already employed, nothing short of
a complete system of values in which every want of every
person or group has a definite place is necessary to provide an
answer.

   In fact, as planning becomes more and more extensive, it
becomes regularly necessary to qualify legal provisions increasingly
by reference to what is ' " fair " or " reasonable " ; this means
that it becomes necessary to leave the decision of the concrete
case more and more to the discretion of the judge or authority
in question.   One could write a history of the decline of the
Rule of Law, the disappearance of the *Rechtsstaat*, in terms
of the progressive introduction of these vague formulæ into
legislation and jurisdiction, and of the increasing arbitrariness
and uncertainty of, and the consequent disrespect for, the law
and the judicature, which in these circumstances could not but
become an instrument of policy.   It is important to point out
once more in this connection that this process of the decline of
the Rule of Law had been going on steadily in Germany for some
time before Hitler came into power, and that a policy well
advanced towards totalitarian planning had already done a great
deal of the work which Hitler completed.

   There can be no doubt that planning necessarily involves

deliberate discrimination between particular needs of different people, and allowing one man to do what another must be prevented from doing. It must lay down by a legal rule how well off particular people shall be and what different people are to be allowed to have and do. It means in effect a return to the rule of status, a reversal of the " movement of progressive societies " which, in the famous phrase of Sir Henry Maine, " has hitherto been a movement from status to contract ". Indeed, the Rule of Law, more than the rule of contract, should probably be regarded as the true opposite of the rule of status. It is the Rule of Law, in the sense of the rule of formal law, the absence of legal privileges of particular people designated by authority, which safeguards that equality before the law which is the opposite of arbitrary government.

* * * * *

A necessary, and only apparently paradoxical, result of this is that formal equality before the law is in conflict, and in fact incompatible, with any activity of the government deliberately aiming at material or substantive equality of different people, and that any policy aiming at a substantive ideal of distributive justice must lead to the destruction of the Rule of Law. To produce the same result for different people it is necessary to treat them differently. To give different people the same objective opportunities is not to give them the same subjective chance. It cannot be denied that the Rule of Law produces economic inequality— all that can be claimed for it is that this inequality is not designed to affect particular people in a particular way. It is very significant and characteristic that socialists (and Nazis) have always protested against " merely " formal justice, that they have always objected to a law which had no views on how well off particular people ought to be,[1] and that they have always demanded a " socialisation of the law ", attacked the independence of judges, and at the same time given their support to all such movements as the *Freirechtsschule* which undermined the Rule of Law.

It may even be said that for the Rule of Law to be effective it is more important that there should be a rule applied always without exceptions, than what this rule is. Often the content of the rule is indeed of minor importance, provided the same rule is universally enforced. To revert to a former example : it does

[1] It is therefore not altogether false when the legal theorist of National-Socialism, Carl Schmitt, opposes to the liberal *Rechtsstaat* (i.e. the Rule of Law) the national-socialist ideal of the *gerechte Staat* (the just state)—only that the sort of justice which is opposed to formal justice necessarily implies discrimination between persons.

not matter whether we all drive on the left- or on the right-hand side of the road so long as we all do the same.   The important thing is that the rule enables us to predict other people's behaviour correctly, and this requires that it should apply to all cases—even if in a particular instance we feel it to be unjust.

The conflict between formal justice and formal equality before the law on the one hand, and the attempts to realise various ideals of substantive justice and equality on the other, also accounts for the widespread confusion about the concept of " privilege " and its consequent abuse.   To mention only the most important instance of this abuse—the application of the term privilege to property as such.   It would indeed be privilege if, for example, as has sometimes been the case in the past, landed property were reserved to members of the nobility.   And it is privilege if, as is true in our time, the right to produce or sell particular things is reserved to particular people designated by authority.   But to call private property as such, which all can acquire under the same rules, a privilege, because only some succeed in acquiring it, is depriving the word privilege of its meaning.

The unpredictability of the particular effects, which is the distinguishing characteristic of the formal laws of a liberal system, is also important because it helps us to clear up another confusion about the nature of this system : the belief that its characteristic attitude is inaction of the state.   The question whether the state should or should not " act " or " interfere " poses an altogether false alternative, and the term *laissez-faire* is a highly ambiguous and misleading description of the principles on which a liberal policy is based.   Of course, every state must act and every action of the state interferes with something or other.   But that is not the point.   The important question is whether the individual can foresee the action of the state and make use of this knowledge as a datum in forming his own plans, with the result that the state cannot control the use made of its machinery, and that the individual knows precisely how far he will be protected against interference from others, or whether the state is in a position to frustrate individual efforts.   The state controlling weights and measures (or preventing fraud and deception in any other way) is certainly acting, while the state permitting the use of violence, for example, by strike pickets, is inactive.   Yet it is in the first case that the state observes liberal principles and in the second that it does not.   Similarly with respect to most of the general and permanent rules which the state may establish with regard to production, such as building regulations or factory laws : these may be wise or unwise in the particular instance, but they do not conflict with liberal principles so long as they are intended to be permanent and are not used to favour or harm particular people.

It is true that in these instances there will, apart from the long-run effects which cannot be predicted, also be short-run effects on particular people which may be clearly known.   But with this kind of laws the short-run effects are in general not (or at least ought not to be) the guiding consideration.   As these immediate and predictable effects become more important compared with the long-run effects, we approach the border-line where the distinction, however, clear in principle, becomes blurred in practice.

*   *   *   *   *

The Rule of Law was consciously evolved only during the liberal age and is one of its greatest achievements, not only as a safeguard but as the legal embodiment of freedom.   As Immanuel Kant put it (and Voltaire expressed it before him in very much the same terms), " Man is free if he needs to obey no person but solely the laws ".   As a vague ideal it has, however, existed at least since Roman times, and during the last few centuries it has never been as seriously threatened as it is to-day.   The idea that there is no limit to the powers of the legislator is in part a result of popular sovereignty and democratic government.   It has been strengthened by the belief that so long as all actions of the state are duly authorised by legislation, the Rule of Law will be preserved.   But this is completely to misconceive the meaning of the Rule of Law.   This rule has little to do with the question whether all actions of government are legal in the juridical sense. They may well be and yet not conform to the Rule of Law. The fact that somebody has full legal authority to act in the way he does gives no answer to the question whether the law gives him power to act arbitrarily or whether the law prescribes unequivocally how he has to act.   It may well be that Hitler has obtained his unlimited powers in a strictly constitutional manner and that whatever he does is therefore legal in the juridical sense. But who would suggest for that reason that the Rule of Law still prevails in Germany ?

To say that in a planned society the Rule of Law cannot hold is, therefore, not to say that the actions of the government will not be legal or that such a society will necessarily be lawless.   It means only that the use of the government's coercive powers will no longer be limited and determined by pre-established rules. The law can, and to make a central direction of economic activity possible must, legalise what to all intents and purposes remains arbitrary action.   If the law says that such a Board or Authority may do what it pleases, anything that Board or Authority does is legal—but its actions are certainly not subject to the Rule of Law. By giving the government unlimited powers the most arbitrary rule can be made legal : and in this way a democracy may set up the most complete despotism imaginable.[1]

If, however, the law is to enable authorities to direct economic life, it must give them powers to make and enforce decisions in circumstances which cannot be foreseen and on principles which cannot be stated in generic form. The consequence is that as planning extends, the delegation of legislative powers to divers Boards and Authorities becomes increasingly common. When before the last war, in a case to which the late Lord Hewart has recently drawn attention, Mr. Justice Darling said " that Parliament had enacted only last year that the Board of Agriculture in acting as they did should be no more impeachable than Parliament itself ", this was still a rare thing. It has since become an almost daily occurrence. Constantly the broadest powers are conferred on new authorities which, without being bound by fixed rules, have almost unlimited discretion in regulating this or that activity of the people.

The Rule of Law thus implies limits to the scope of legislation : it restricts it to the kind of general rules known as formal law, and excludes legislation either directly aimed at particular people, or at enabling anybody to use the coercive power of the state for the purpose of such discrimination. It means, not that everything is regulated by law, but, on the contrary, that the coercive power of the state can be used only in cases defined in advance by the law and in such a way that it can be foreseen how it will be used. A particular enactment can thus infringe the Rule of Law. Anyone ready to deny this would have to contend that whether the Rule of Law prevails to-day in Germany, Italy, or Russia, depends on whether the dictators have obtained their absolute power by constitutional means.[2]

* * * * *

[1] The conflict is thus *not*, as it has often been misconceived in nineteenth-century discussions, one between liberty and law. As John Locke had already made clear, there can be no liberty without law. The conflict is between different kinds of law, law so different that it should hardly be called by the same name : one is the law of the Rule of Law, general principles laid down beforehand, the " rules of the game " which enable individuals to foresee how the coercive apparatus of the state will be used, or what he and his fellow-citizens will be allowed to do, or made to do, in stated circumstances. The other kind of law gives in effect the authority power to do what it thinks fit to do. Thus the Rule of Law could clearly not be preserved in a democracy that undertook to decide every conflict of interests not according to rules previously laid down, but " on its merits ".

[2] Another illustration of an infringement of the Rule of Law by legislation is the case of the bill of attainder, familiar in the history of this country. The form which the Rule of Law takes in criminal law is usually expressed by the Latin tag *nulla poena sine lege*—no punishment without a law expressly prescribing it. The essence of this rule is that the law must have existed as a general rule before the individual case arose to which it is to be applied. Nobody would argue that, when in a famous case in Henry VIII's reign Parlia-

Whether, as in some countries, the main applications of the Rule of Law are laid down in a Bill of Rights or a Constitutional Code, or whether the principle is merely a firmly established tradition, matters comparatively little.   But it will readily be seen that whatever form it takes, any such recognised limitations of the powers of legislation imply the recognition of the inalienable right of the individual, inviolable rights of man.

It is pathetic, but characteristic of the muddle into which many of our intellectuals have been led by the conflicting ideals in which they believe, that a leading advocate of the most comprehensive central planning like Mr. H. G. Wells should at the same time write an ardent defence of the Rights of Man.   The individual rights which Mr. Wells hopes to preserve would inevitably obstruct the planning which he desires.   To some extent he seems to realise the dilemma, and we find therefore the provisions of his proposed " Declaration of the Rights of Man " so hedged about with qualifications that they lose all significance. While, for instance, his Declaration proclaims that every man " shall have the right to buy and sell without any discriminatory restrictions anything which may be lawfully bought and sold ", which is admirable, he immediately proceeds to make the whole provision nugatory by adding that it applies only to buying and selling " in such quantities and with such reservations as are compatible with the common welfare ".   But since, of course, all restrictions ever imposed upon buying or selling anything are supposed to be necessary in the interest of the " common welfare ", there is really no restriction which this clause effectively prevents, and no right of the individual that is safeguarded by it.   Or, to take another basic clause, the Declaration states that every man " may engage in any lawful occupation " and that " he is entitled to paid employment and to a free choice whenever there is any variety of employment open to him ".   It is not stated, however, who is to decide whether a particular employment is " open " to a particular person, and the added provision that " he may suggest employment for himself and have his claim publicly

ment resolved with respect to the Bishop of Rochester's cook " that the said Richard Rose shall be boiled to death without having the advantage of his clergy ", this act was performed under the Rule of Law.   But while the Rule of Law had become an essential part of criminal procedure in all liberal countries, it cannot be preserved in totalitarian regimes.   There, as E. B. Ashton has well expressed it, the liberal maxim is replaced by the principles *nullum crimen sine poena*—no " crime " must remain without punishment, whether the law explicitly provides for it or not.   " The rights of the state do not end with punishing law breakers.   The community is entitled to whatever may seem necessary to the protection of its interests—of which observance of the law, as it stands, is only one of the more elementary requirements " (E. B. Ashton, *The Fascist, His State and Mind*, 1937, p. 119).   What is an infringement of " the interests of the community " is, of course, decided by the authorities.

considered, accepted or dismissed " shows that Mr. Wells is thinking in terms of an authority which decides whether a man is " entitled " to a particular position—which certainly means the opposite of free choice of occupation. And how in a planned world " freedom of travel and migration " is to be secured when not only the means of communication and currencies are controlled, but also the location of industries planned, or how the freedom of the press is to be safeguarded when the supply of paper and all the channels of distribution are controlled by the planning authority, are questions to which Mr. Wells provides as little answer as any other planner.

In this respect much more consistency is shown by the more numerous reformers who, ever since the beginning of the socialist movement, have attacked the " metaphysical " idea of individual rights and insisted that in a rationally ordered world there will be no individual rights but only individual duties. This, indeed, has become the much more common attitude of our so-called progressives, and few things are more certain to expose one to the reproach of being a reactionary than if one protests against a measure on the grounds that it is a violation of the rights of the individual. Even a liberal paper like *The Economist* was a few years ago holding up to us the example of the French, of all people, who had learnt the lesson

> that democratic government no less than dictatorship must always [*sic*] have plenary powers *in posse*, without sacrificing their democratic and representative character. There is no restrictive penumbra of individual rights that can never be touched by government in administrative matters whatever the circumstances. There is no limit to the power of ruling which can and should be taken by a government freely chosen by the people and can be fully and openly criticised by an opposition.

This may be inevitable in wartime when, of course, even free and open criticism is necessarily restricted. But the " always " in the statement quoted does not suggest that *The Economist* regards it as a regrettable wartime necessity. Yet as a permanent institution this view is certainly incompatible with the preservation of the Rule of Law, and it leads straight to the totalitarian state. It is, however, the view which all those who want the government to direct economic life must hold.

How even a formal recognition of individual rights, or of the equal rights of minorities, loses all significance in a state which embarks on a complete control of economic life, has been amply demonstrated by the experience of the various Central European countries. It has been shown there that it is possible to pursue a policy of ruthless discrimination against national minorities by the use of recognised instruments of economic policy, without ever infringing the letter of the statutory protection of minority rights. This oppression by means of economic policy was greatly facilitated by the fact that particular industries or activities were largely in the hands of a national minority so that many a measure aimed ostensibly against an industry or class was in fact aimed at a national minority. But the almost boundless possibilities for a policy of discrimination and oppression provided by such apparently innocuous principles as " government control of the development of industries " have been amply demonstrated to all those desirous of seeing how the political consequences of planning appear in practice.

CHAPTER VII

ECONOMIC CONTROL AND TOTALITARIANISM

> The control of the production of wealth is the control of human life itself.
>
> *Hilaire Belloc.*

MOST planners who have seriously considered the practical aspects of their task have little doubt that a directed economy must be run on more or less dictatorial lines. That the complex system of interrelated activities, if it is to be consciously directed at all, must be directed by a single staff of experts, and that ultimate responsibility and power must rest in the hands of a commander-in-chief, whose actions must not be fettered by democratic procedure, is too obvious a consequence of under-lying ideas of central planning not to command fairly general assent. The consolation our planners offer us is that this authoritarian direction will apply " only " to economic matters. One of the most prominent American planners, Mr. Stuart Chase, assures us, for instance, that in a planned society " political democracy can remain if it confines itself to all but economic matter ". Such assurances are usually accompanied by the suggestion that by giving up freedom in what are, or ought to be, the less important aspects of our lives, we shall obtain greater freedom in the pursuit of higher values. On this ground people who abhor the idea of a political dictatorship often clamour for a dictator in the economic field.

The arguments used appeal to our best instincts and often attract the finest minds. If planning really did free us from the less important cares and so made it easier to render our existence one of plain living and high thinking, who would wish to belittle such an ideal ? If our economic activities really concerned only the inferior or even more sordid sides of life, of course we ought to endeavour by all means to find a way to relieve ourselves from the excessive care for material ends, and, leaving them to be cared for by some piece of utilitarian machinery, set our minds free for the higher things of life.

Unfortunately the assurance people derive from this belief that the power which is exercised over economic life is a power over matters of secondary importance only, and which makes them take lightly the threat to the freedom of our economic pursuits, is altogether unwarranted. It is largely a consequence of the erroneous belief that there are purely economic ends separate from the other ends of life. Yet, apart from the pathological case of the miser, there is no such thing. The ultimate ends of the activities of reasonable beings are never economic. Strictly speaking there is no " economic motive " but only economic factors conditioning our striving for other ends. What in ordinary language is misleadingly called the " economic motive " means merely the desire for general opportunity, the desire for power to achieve unspecified ends.[1] If we strive for money it is because it offers us the widest choice in enjoying the fruits of our efforts. Because in modern society it is through the limitation of our money incomes that we are made to feel the restrictions which our relative poverty still imposes upon us, many have come to hate money as the symbol of these restrictions. But this is to mistake for the cause the medium through which a force makes itself felt. It would be much truer to say that money is one of the greatest instruments of freedom ever invented by man. It is money which in existing society opens an astounding range of choice to the poor man, a range greater than that which not many generations ago was open to the wealthy. We shall better understand the significance of this service of money if we consider what it would really mean if, as so many socialists characteristically propose, the " pecuniary motive " were largely displaced by " non-economic incentives ". If all rewards, instead of being offered in money, were offered in the form of public distinctions or privileges, positions of power over other men, or better housing or better food, opportunities for travel or education, this would merely mean that the recipient would no longer be allowed to choose, and that, whoever fixed the reward, determined not only its size but also the particular form in which it should be enjoyed.

*   *   *   *   *

Once we realise that there is no separate economic motive and that an economic gain or economic loss is merely a gain or a loss where it is still in our power to decide which of our needs or desires shall be affected, it is also easier to see the important kernel of truth in the general belief that economic matters affect only the less important ends of life, and to understand the contempt in which " merely " economic considerations are often held. In a sense this is quite justified in a market economy—but only in such a free economy. So long as we can freely dispose over our income and all our possessions, economic loss will always deprive us only of what we regard as the least important of the desires we were able to satisfy. A " merely " economic loss is thus one whose effect we can still make fall on our less important needs, while when we say that

[1] Cf. L. Robbins, *The Economic Causes of War*, 1939, Appendix.

the value of something we have lost is much greater than its economic value, or that it cannot even be estimated in economic terms, this means that we must bear the loss where it falls. And similarly with an economic gain. Economic changes, in other words, usually affect only the fringe, the " margin ", of our needs. There are many things which are more important than anything which economic gains or losses are likely to affect, which for us stand high above the amenities and even above many of the necessities of life which are affected by the economic ups and downs. Compared with them, the " filthy lucre ", the question whether we are economically somewhat worse or better off, seems of little importance. This makes many people believe that anything which, like economic planning, affects only our economic interests, cannot seriously interfere with the more basic values of life.

This, however, is an erroneous conclusion. Economic values are less important to us than many things precisely because in economic matters we are free to decide what to us is more, and what less, important. Or, as we might say, because in the present society it is *we* who have to solve the economic problems of our lives. To be controlled in our economic pursuits means to be always controlled unless we declare our specific purpose. Or, since when we declare our specific purpose we shall also have to get it approved, we should really be controlled in everything.

The question raised by economic planning is, therefore, not merely whether we shall be able to satisfy what we regard as our more or less important needs in the way we prefer. It is whether it shall be we who decide what is more, and what is less, important for us, or whether this is to be decided by the planner. Economic planning would not affect merely those of our marginal needs that we have in mind when we speak contemptuously about the merely economic. It would, in effect, mean that we as individuals should no longer be allowed to decide what we regard as marginal.

The authority directing all economic activity would control not merely the part of our lives which is concerned with inferior things ; it would control the allocation of the limited means for all our ends. And whoever controls all economic activity controls the means for all our ends, and must therefore decide which are to be satisfied and which not. This is really the crux of the matter. Economic control is not merely control of a sector of human life which can be separated from the rest ; it is the control of the means for all our ends. And whoever has sole control of the means must also determine which ends are to be served, which values are to be rated higher and which lower, in short, what men should believe and strive for.   Central planning means that the economic problem is to be solved by the community instead of by the individual ; but this involves that it must also be the community, or rather its representatives, who must decide the relative importance of the different needs.

The so-called economic freedom which the planners promise us means precisely that we are to be relieved of the necessity of solving our own economic problems and that the bitter choices which this often involves are to be made for us.   Since under modern conditions we are for almost everything dependent on means which our fellow men provide, economic planning would involve direction of almost the whole of our life.   There is hardly an aspect of it, from our primary needs to our relations with our family and friends, from the nature of our work to the use of our leisure, over which the planner would not exercise his " conscious control ".[1]

*   *   *   *   *

The power of the planner over our private lives would be no less complete if he chose not to exercise it by direct control of our consumption.   Although a planned society would probably to some extent employ rationing and similar devices, the power of the planner over our private lives does not depend on this, and would be hardly less effective if the consumer were nominally free to spend his income as he pleased.   The source of this power over all consumption which in a planned society the authority would possess would be their control over production.

Our freedom of choice in a competitive society rests on the fact that, if one person refuses to satisfy our wishes we can turn to another.   But if we face a monopolist we are at his mercy. And an authority directing the whole economic system would be the most powerful monopolist conceivable.   While we need probably not be afraid that such an authority would exploit this power in the manner in which a private monopolist would do so, while its purpose would presumably not be the extortion of

[1] The extent of the control over all life that economic control confers is nowhere better illustrated than in the field of foreign exchanges.   Nothing would at first seem to affect private life less than a state control of the dealings in foreign exchange, and most people will regard its introduction with complete indifference.   Yet the experience of most continental countries has taught thoughtful people to regard this step as the decisive advance on the path to totalitarianism and the suppression of individual liberty.   It is in fact the complete delivery of the individual to the tyranny of the state, the final suppression of all means of escape—not merely for the rich, but for everybody.   Once the individual is no longer free to travel, no longer free to buy foreign books or journals, once all the means of foreign contact can be restricted to those of whom official opinion approves or for whom it is regarded as necessary, the effective control of opinion is much greater than that ever exercised by any of the absolutist governments of the seventeenth and eighteenth centuries.

maximum financial gain, it would have complete power to decide what we are to be given and on what terms. It would not only decide what commodities and services were to be available, and in what quantities; it would be able to direct their distribution between districts and groups and could, if it wished, discriminate between persons to any degree it liked. If we remember why planning is advocated by most people, can there be much doubt that this power would be used for the ends of which the authority approves and to prevent the pursuits of ends which it disapproves?

The power conferred by the control of production and prices is almost unlimited. In a competitive society the prices we have to pay for a thing, the rate at which we can get one thing for another, depend on the quantities of other things of which, by taking one, we deprive the other members of society. This price is not determined by the conscious will of anybody. And if one way of achieving our ends proves too expensive for us, we are free to try other ways. The obstacles in our path are not due to somebody disapproving of our ends, but to the fact that the same means are also wanted elsewhere. In a directed economy, where the authority watches over the ends pursued, it is certain that it would use its powers to assist some ends and to prevent the realisation of others. Not our own view, but somebody else's, of what we ought to like or dislike would determine what we should get. And since the authority would have the power to thwart any efforts to elude its guidance, it would control what we consume almost as effectively as if it directly told us how to spend our income.

*   *   *   *   *

Not only in our capacity as consumers, however, and not even mainly in that capacity, would the will of the authority shape and " guide " our daily lives. It would do so even more in our position as producers. These two aspects of our lives cannot be separated; and as for most of us the time we spend at our work is a large part of our whole lives, and as our job usually also determines the place where and the people among whom we live, some freedom in choosing our work is, probably, even more important for our happiness than freedom to spend our income during the hours of leisure.

No doubt it is true that even in the best of worlds this freedom will be very limited. Few people have ever an abundance of choice of occupation. But what matters is that we have some choice, that we are not absolutely tied to a particular job which has been chosen for us, or which we may have chosen in the past, and that if one position becomes quite intolerable, or if we set our heart on another, there is almost always a way for the able, some sacrifice at the price of which he may achieve his goal. Nothing makes conditions more unbearable than the knowledge that no effort of ours can change them ; and even if we should never have the strength of mind to make the necessary sacrifice, the knowledge that we could escape if we only strove hard enough makes many otherwise intolerable positions bearable.

This is not to say that in this respect all is for the best in our present world, or has been so in the most liberal past, and that there is not much that could be done to improve the opportunities of choice open to the people. Here as elsewhere the state can do a great deal to help the spreading of knowledge and information and to assist mobility. But the point is that the kind of state action which really would increase opportunity is almost precisely the opposite of the " planning " which is now generally advocated and practised. Most planners, it is true, promise that in the new planned world free choice of occupation will be scrupulously preserved or even increased. But there they promise more than they can possibly fulfil. If they want to plan they must control the entry into the different trades and occupations, or the terms of remuneration, or both. In almost all known instances of planning the establishment of such controls and restrictions was among the first measures taken. If such control were universally practised and exercised by a single planning authority, one needs little imagination to see what would become of the " free choice of occupation " promised. The " freedom of choice " would be purely fictitious, a mere promise to practise no discrimination where in the nature of the case discrimination must be practised, and where all one could hope would be that the selection would be made on what the authority believed to be objective grounds.

There would be little difference if the planning authority confined itself to fixing the terms of employment and tried to regulate numbers by adjusting these terms. By prescribing the remuneration it would no less effectively bar groups of people from entering many trades than by specifically excluding them. A rather plain girl who badly wants to become a saleswoman, a weakly boy who has set his heart on a job where his weakness handicaps him, as well as in general the apparently less able or less suitable are not necessarily excluded in a competitive society ; if they value the position sufficiently, they will frequently be able to get a start by a financial sacrifice and will later make good through qualities which at first are not so obvious. But when the authority fixes the remuneration for a whole category and the selection among the candidates is made by an objective test, the strength of their desire for the job will count for very little. The person whose qualifications are not of the standard type, or whose temperament is not of the ordinary kind, will no longer be able to come to special arrangements with an employer whose dispositions will fit in with his special needs : the person who prefers irregular hours or even a happy-go-lucky existence with a small and perhaps uncertain income to a regular routine will no longer have the choice. Conditions will be without exception what in some measure they inevitably are in a large organisation—or rather worse, because there will be no possibility of escape. We shall no longer be free to be rational or efficient only when and where we think it worth while, we shall all have to conform to the standards which the planning authority must fix in order to simplify its task. To make this immense task manageable it will have to reduce the diversity of human capacities and inclinations to a few categories of readily interchangeable units and deliberately to disregard minor personal differences. Although the professed aim of planning would be that man should cease to be a mere means, in fact—since it would be impossible to take account in the plan of individual likes and dislikes—the individual would more than ever become a mere means, to be used by the authority in the service of such abstractions as the " social welfare " or the " good of the community ".

*   *   *   *   *

That in a competitive society most things can be had at a price—though it is often a cruelly high price we have to pay, is a fact the importance of which can hardly be overrated. The alternative is not, however, complete freedom of choice, but orders and prohibitions which must be obeyed and, in the last resort, the favour of the mighty.

It is significant of the confusion prevailing on all these subjects that it should have become a cause for reproach that in a competitive society almost everything can be had at a price. If the people who protest against the higher values of life being brought into the " cash nexus " that we should not be allowed to sacrifice our lesser needs in order to preserve the higher values, and that the choice should be made for us, this demand must be regarded as rather peculiar and scarcely testifies to great respect for the dignity of the individual. That life and health, beauty and virtue, honour and peace of mind, can often be preserved only at considerable material cost, and that somebody must make the choice, is as undeniable as that we all are sometimes not prepared to make the material sacrifices necessary to protect those higher values against all injury. To take only one example : we could, of course, reduce casualties by motor accidents to zero if we were willing to bear the cost—if in no other way—by abolishing motor-cars. And the same is true of thousands of other instances in which we are constantly risking life and health and all the fine values of the spirit, of ourselves and of our fellow men, to further what we at the same time contemptuously describe as our material comfort. Nor can it be otherwise since all our ends compete for the same means; and we could not strive for anything but these absolute values if they were on no account to be endangered.

That people should wish to be relieved of the bitter choice which hard facts often impose upon them is not surprising. But few want to be relieved through the choice being made for them by others. People just wish that the choice should not be necessary at all. And they are only too ready to believe that the choice is not really necessary, that it is imposed upon them merely by the particular economic system under which we live. What they resent is in truth that there is an economic problem.

In their wishful belief that there is really no longer an economic problem people have been confirmed by irresponsible talk about " potential plenty "—which, if it were a fact, would indeed mean that there is no economic problem which makes the choice inevitable. But although this snare has served socialist propaganda under various names as long as socialism has existed, it is still as palpably untrue as it was when it was first used over a hundred years ago. In all this time not one of the many people who have used it has produced a workable plan of how production could be increased so as to abolish even in Western Europe what we regard as poverty—not to speak of the world as a whole. The reader may take it that whoever talks about potential plenty is either dishonest or does not know what he is talking about.[1] Yet it is this false hope as much as anything which drives us along the road to planning.

---

[1] To justify these strong words the following conclusions may be quoted at which Mr. Colin Clark, one of the best known among the younger economic statisticians, and a man of undoubted progressive views and a strictly scientific outlook, has arrived in his *Conditions of Economic Progress* (1940, pp. 3-4) : The " oft-repeated phrases about poverty in the midst of plenty, and the problems of production having already been solved if only we understood the problem of distribution, turn out to be the most untruthful of all modern clichés. . . . The under-utilisation of productive capacity is a question of considerable importance only in the U.S.A., though in certain years also it has been of some importance in Great Britain, Germany and France, but for most of the world it is entirely subsidiary to the more important fact that, with productive resources fully employed, they can produce so little. The age of plenty will still be a long while in coming. . . . If preventable unemployment were eliminated throughout the trade cycle, this would mean a distinct improvement in the standard of living of the population of the U.S.A., but from the standpoint of the world as a whole it would only make a small contribution towards the much greater problem of raising the real income of the bulk of the world population to anything like a civilised standard."

While the popular movement still profits by this false belief, the claim that a planned economy would produce a substantially larger output than the competitive system is being progressively abandoned by most students of the problem. Even a good many economists with socialist views who have seriously studied the problems of central planning are now content to hope that a planned society will equal the efficiency of a competitive system ; they advocate planning no longer because of its superior productivity but because it will enable us to secure a more just and equitable distribution of wealth. This is, indeed, the only argument for planning which can be seriously pressed. It is indisputable that if we want to secure a distribution of wealth which conforms to some predetermined standard, if we want consciously to decide who is to have what, we must plan the whole economic system. But the question remains whether the price we should have to pay for the realisation of somebody's ideal of justice is not bound to be more discontent and more oppression than was ever caused by the much abused free play of economic forces.

*   *   *   *   *

We should be seriously deceiving ourselves if for these apprehensions we sought comfort in the consideration that the adoption of central planning would merely mean a return, after a brief spell of a free economy, to the ties and regulations which have governed economic activity through most ages, and that, therefore, the infringements of personal liberty need not be greater than they were before the age of *laissez-faire*. This is a dangerous illusion. Even during the periods of European history when the regimentation of economic life went furthest, it amounted to little more than the creation of a general and semi-permanent framework of rules within which the individual preserved a wide free sphere. The apparatus of control then available would not have been adequate to impose more than very general directions. And even where the control was most complete it extended only to those activities of a person through which he took part in the social division of labour. In the much wider sphere in which he then still lived on his own products he was free to act as he chose.

The situation is now entirely different. During the liberal era the progressive division of labour has created a situation where almost every one of our activities is part of a social process. This is a development which we cannot reverse since it is only because of it that we can maintain the vastly increased population at anything like present standards. But, in consequence, the substitution of central planning for competition would require central direction of a much greater part of our lives than was ever attempted before. It could not stop at what we regard as our economic activities, because we are now for almost every part of our lives dependent on somebody else's economic activities.[1] The passion for the " collective satisfaction of our needs ", with which our socialists have so well prepared the way for totalitarianism, and which wants us to take our pleasures as well as our necessities at the appointed time and in the prescribed form, is, of course, partly intended as a means of political education. But it is also the result of the exigencies of planning, which consists essentially in depriving us of choice, in order to give us whatever fits best into the plan and that at a time determined by the plan.

It is often said that political freedom is meaningless without economic freedom. This is true enough, but in a sense almost opposite from that in which the phrase is used by our planners. The economic freedom which is the prerequisite of any other freedom cannot be the freedom from economic care which the socialists promise us and which can be obtained only by relieving the individual at the same time of the necessity and of the power of choice ; it must be the freedom of our economic activity which, with the right of choice, inevitably also carries the risk and the responsibility of that right.

[1] It is no accident that in the totalitarian countries, be it Russia or Germany or Italy, the question of how to organise the people's leisure should have become a problem of planning. The Germans have even invented for this problem the horrible and self-contradictory name of *Freizeitgestaltung* (literally : the shaping of the use made of the people's free time) as if it were still," free time " when it has to be spent in the way ordained by authority.

CHAPTER VIII

WHO, WHOM ?

> The finest opportunity ever given to the world was thrown away because the passion for equality made vain the hope for freedom.
>
> *Lord Acton.*

IT is significant that one of the commonest objections to competition is that it is " blind ". It is not irrelevant to recall that to the ancients blindness was an attribute of their deity of justice. Although competition and justice may have little else in common, it is as much a commendation of competition as of justice that it is no respecter of persons. That it is impossible to foretell who will be the lucky ones or whom disaster will strike, that rewards and penalties are not shared out according to somebody's views about the merits or demerits of different people, but depend on their capacity and their luck, is as important as that in framing legal rules we should not be able to predict which particular person will gain and which will lose by their application. And this is none the less true because in competition chance and good luck are often as important as skill and foresight in determining the fate of different people.

The choice open to us is not between a system in which everybody will get what he deserves according to some absolute and universal standard of right, and one where the individual shares are determined partly by accident or good or ill chance, but between a system where it is the will of a few persons that decides who is to get what, and one where it depends at least partly on the ability and enterprise of the people concerned and partly on unforeseeable circumstances. This is no less relevant because in a system of free enterprise chances are not equal, since such a system is necessarily based on private property and (though perhaps not with the same necessity) on inheritance, with the differences in opportunity which these create. There is indeed a strong case for reducing this inequality of opportunity as far as congenital differences permit and as it is possible to do so without destroying the impersonal character of the process by which everybody has to take his chance and no person's view about what is right and desirable overrules that of others.

The fact that the opportunities open to the poor in a competitive society are much more restricted than those open to the rich does not make it less true that in such a society the poor are much more free than a person commanding much greater material comfort in a different type of society. Although under competition the probability that a man who starts poor will reach great wealth is much smaller than is true of the man who has inherited property, it is not only possible for the former, but the competitive system is the only one where it depends solely on him and not on the favours of the mighty, and where nobody can prevent a man from attempting to achieve this result. It is only because we have forgotten what unfreedom means that we often overlook the patent fact that in every real sense a badly paid unskilled worker in this country has more freedom to shape his life than many a small entrepreneur in Germany or a much better paid engineer or manager in Russia. Whether it is a question of changing his job or the place where he lives, of professing certain views or of spending his leisure in a particular manner, although sometimes the price he may have to pay for following his inclinations may be high, and to many appear too high, there are no absolute impediments, no dangers to bodily security and freedom that confine him by brute force to the task and the environment to which a superior has assigned him.

That the ideal of justice of most socialists would be satisfied if merely private income from property were abolished and the differences between the earned incomes of different people remained what they are now, is true.[1] What these people forget is that in transferring all property in the means of production to the state they put the state in a position whereby its action must in effect decide all other incomes. The power thus given to the state and the demand that the state should use it to " plan " means nothing else than that it should use it in full awareness of all these effects.

To believe that the power which is thus conferred on the state is merely transferred to it from others is erroneous. It is a power which is newly created and which in a competitive society nobody possesses. So long as property is divided among many owners, none of them acting independently has exclusive power

---

[1] It is probable that we habitually overestimate the extent to which inequality of incomes is mainly caused by income derived from property, and therefore the extent to which the major inequalities would be abolished by abolishing income from property. What little information we have about the distribution of incomes in Soviet Russia does not suggest that the inequalities are there substantially smaller than in a capitalist society. Max Eastman (*The End of Socialism in Russia*, 1937, pp. 30–4) gives some information from official Russian sources which suggest that the difference between the highest and the lowest salaries paid in Russia is of the same order of magnitude (about 50 to 1) as in the United States ; and Leon Trotsky, according to an article quoted by James Burnham (*The Managerial Revolution*, 1941, p. 43), estimated as late as 1939 that " the upper 11 or 12 per cent. of the Soviet population now receives approximately 50 per cent. of the national income. This differentiation is sharper than in the United States, where the upper 10 per cent. of the population receives approximately 35 per cent. of the national income."

to determine the income and position of particular people—nobody is tied to him except by the fact that he may offer better terms than anybody else.

What our generation has forgotten is that the system of private property is the most important guarantee of freedom, not only for those who own property, but scarcely less for those who do not.   It is only because the control of the means of production is divided among many people acting independently that nobody has complete power over us, that we as individuals can decide what to do with ourselves.   If all the means of production were vested in a single hand, whether it be nominally that of " society " as a whole, or that of a dictator, whoever exercises this control has complete power over us.   Who can seriously doubt that a member of a small racial or religious minority will be freer with no property so long as fellow members of his community have property and are therefore able to employ him, than he would be if private property were abolished and he became owner of a nominal share in the communal property.   Or that the power which a multiple millionaire, who may be my neighbour and perhaps my employer, has over me is very much less than that which the smallest *fonctionaire* possesses who wields the coercive power of the state and on whose discretion it depends whether and how I am to be allowed to live or to work ?   And who will deny that a world in which the wealthy are powerful is still a better world than one in which only the already powerful can acquire wealth ?

It is pathetic, yet at the same time encouraging, to find as prominent an old communist as Mr. Max Eastman rediscovering this truth :

> It seems obvious to me now [he writes in a recent article]—though I have been slow, I must say, in coming to the conclusion—that the institution of private property is one of the main things that have given man that limited amount of free and equalness that Marx hoped to render infinite by abolishing this institution.   Strangely enough Marx was the first to see this.   He is the one who informed us, looking backwards, that the evolution of private capitalism with its free market had been a precondition for the evolution of all our democratic freedoms.   It never occurred to him, looking forward, that if this was so, these other freedoms might disappear with the abolition of the free market.[1]

*   *   *   *   *

It is sometimes said, in answer to such apprehensions, that there is no reason why the planner should determine the incomes of individuals.   The social and political difficulties involved in

---

[1] Max Eastman in *The Reader's Digest*, July 1941, p. 39.

deciding the shares of different people in the national income are so obvious that even the most inveterate planner may well hesitate before he charges any authority with this task. Probably everybody who realises what it involves would prefer to confine planning to production, to use it only to secure a " rational organisation of industry ", leaving the distribution of incomes as far as possible to impersonal forces. Although it is impossible to direct industry without exercising some influence on distribution, and although no planner will wish to leave distribution entirely to the forces of the market, they would probably all prefer to confine themselves to seeing that this distribution conforms to certain general rules of equity and fairness, that extreme inequalities are avoided, and that the relation between the remuneration of the major classes is just, without undertaking the responsibility for the position of particular people within their class, or for the gradations and differentiations between smaller groups and individuals.

We have already seen that the close interdependence of all economic phenomena makes it difficult to stop planning just where we wish, and that, once the free working of the market is impeded beyond a certain degree, the planner will be forced to extend his controls till they become all-comprehensive. These economic considerations, which explain why it is impossible to stop deliberate control just where we should wish, are strongly reinforced by certain social or political tendencies whose strength makes itself increasingly felt as planning extends.

Once it becomes increasingly true, and is generally recognised, that the position of the individual is determined not by impersonal forces, not as a result of the competitive effort of many, but by the deliberate decision of authority, the attitude of the people towards their position in the social order necessarily changes. There will always exist inequalities which will appear unjust to those who suffer from them, disappointments which will appear unmerited, and strokes of misfortune which those hit have not deserved. But when these things occur in a society which is consciously directed, the way in which people will react will be very different from what it is when they are nobody's conscious choice. Inequality is undoubtedly more readily borne, and affects the dignity of the person much less, if it is determined by impersonal forces, than when it is due to design. In a competitive society it is no slight to a person, no offence to his dignity, to be told by any particular firm that it has no need for his services, or that it cannot offer him a better job. It is true that in periods of prolonged mass-unemployment the effect on many may be very similar. But there are other and better methods to prevent that scourge than central direction. But the unemployment or the loss of income which will always affect some in any society is certainly less degrading if it is the result of misfortune and not deliberately imposed by authority. However bitter the experience, it would be very much worse in a planned society. There individuals will have to decide not whether a person is needed for a particular job, but whether he is of use for anything, and how useful he is. His position in life must be assigned to him by somebody else.

While people will submit to suffering which may hit anyone, they will not so easily submit to suffering which is the result of the decision of authority. It may be bad to be just a cog in an impersonal machine; but it is infinitely worse if we can no longer leave it, if we are tied to our place and to the superiors who have been chosen for us. Dissatisfaction of everybody with his lot will inevitably grow with the consciousness that it is the result of deliberate human decision.

Once government has embarked upon planning for the sake of justice, it cannot refuse responsibility for anybody's fate or position. In a planned society, we shall all know that we are better or worse off than others, not because of circumstances which nobody controls, and which it is impossible to foresee with certainty, but because some authority wills it. And all our efforts directed towards improving our position will have to aim, not at foreseeing and preparing as well as we can for the circumstances over which we have no control, but at influencing in our favour the authority which has all the power. The nightmare of English nineteenth-century political thinkers: the state in which "no avenue to wealth and honour would exist save through the government" [1] would be realised in a completeness which they never imagined—though familiar enough in some countries which have since passed to totalitarianism.

*   *   *   *   *

As soon as the state takes upon itself the task of planning the whole economic life, the problem of the due station of the different individuals and groups must indeed inevitably become the central political problem. As the coercive power of the state will alone decide who is to have what, the only power worth having will be a share in the exercise of this directing power. There will be no economic or social questions that would not be political questions in the sense that their solution will depend exclusively on who wields the coercive power, on whose are the views that will prevail on all occasions.

I believe it was Lenin himself who introduced to Russia the famous phrase "who, whom?"—during the early years of Soviet

[1] The actual words are those of the young Disraeli.

rule the byword in which the people summed up the universal problem of a socialist society.[1] Who plans whom, who directs and dominates whom, who assigns to other people their station in life, and who is to have his due allotted by others ? These become necessarily the central issues to be decided solely by the supreme power.

More recently an American student of politics has enlarged upon Lenin's phrase and asserted that the problem of all government is " who gets what, when, and how ? " In a way this is not untrue. That all government affects the relative position of different people and that there is under any system scarcely an aspect of our lives which may not be affected by government action, is certainly true. In so far as government does anything at all, its action will always have some effect on " who gets what, when, and how ".

There are, however, two fundamental distinctions to be made. Firstly, particular measures may be taken without the knowledge of how they will affect particular individuals, and without aiming at such particular effects. This point we have already discussed. Secondly, it is the extent of the activities of the government which decides whether everything that any person gets at any time depends on the government, or whether its influence is confined to whether some people will get some things in some way at some time. Here lies the whole difference between a free and a totalitarian system.

The contrast between a liberal and a totally planned system is characteristically illustrated by the common complaints of Nazis and socialists of the " artificial separations of economics and politics ", and their equally common demand for the dominance of politics over economics. These phrases presumably mean not only that economic forces are now allowed to work for ends which are not part of the policy of the government, but also that economic power can be used independently of government direction and for ends of which the government may not approve. But the alternative is not merely that there would be only one power, but that this single power, the ruling group, should have control over all human ends, and particularly that it should have complete power over the position of each individual in society.

*   *   *   *   *

That a government which undertakes to direct economic activity will have to use its power to realise somebody's ideal of distributive justice is certain. But how can and how will it use that

[1] Cf. M. Muggeridge, *Winter in Moscow*, 1934 ; A. Feiler, *The Experiment of Bolshevism*, 1930.

power ? By what principles will it or ought it to be guided ? Is there a definite answer to the innumerable questions of relative merits that will arise and which will have to be solved deliberately ? Is there a scale of values on which reasonable people can be expected to agree, which would justify a new hierarchical order of society, and is likely to satisfy the demands for justice ?

There is only one general principle, one simple rule which would indeed provide a definite answer to all these questions : equality, complete and absolute equality of all individuals in all those points which are subject to human control. If this were generally regarded as desirable (quite apart from the question whether it would be practicable, i.e., whether it would provide adequate incentives), it would give the vague idea of distributive justice a clear meaning and would give the planner definite guidance. But nothing is further from the truth than that people in general regard mechanical equality of this kind as desirable. No socialist movement which aimed at complete equality has ever gained substantial support. What socialism promised was not an absolutely equal, but a more just and more equal distribution. Not equality in the absolute sense, but " greater equality " is the only goal which is seriously aimed at.

Though these two ideals sound very similar, they are as different as possible as far as our problem is concerned. While absolute equality would clearly determine the planner's task, the desire for greater equality is merely negative, no more than an expression of dislike of the present state of affairs ; and so long as we are not prepared to say that every move in the direction towards complete equality is desirable, it answers scarcely any of the questions the planner will have to decide.

This is not a quibble about words. We face here a crucial issue which the similarity of the terms used is apt to conceal. While agreement on complete equality would answer all the problems of merit the planner must answer, the formula of the approach to greater equality answers practically none. Its content is hardly more definite than the phrases " common good " or " social welfare ". It does not free us from the necessity of deciding in every particular instance between the merits of particular individuals or groups, and gives us no help in that decision. All it tells us in effect is to take from the rich as much as we can. But when it comes to the distribution of the spoils, the problem is the same as if the formula of " greater equality " had never been conceived.

*   *   *   *   *

Most people find it difficult to admit that we do not possess moral standards which would enable us to settle these questions

—if not perfectly, at least to greater general satisfaction than is done by the competitive system. Have we not all some idea of what is a " just price " or a " fair wage " ? Can we not rely on the strong sense of fairness of the people ? And even if we do not now agree fully on what is just or fair in a particular case, would popular ideas not soon consolidate into more definite standards if people were given an opportunity to see their ideals realised ?

Unfortunately there is little ground for such hopes. What standards we have are derived from the competitive regime we have known, and would necessarily disappear soon after the disappearance of competition. What we mean by a just price, or a fair wage, is either the customary price or wage, the return which past experience has made people expect, or the price or wage that would exist if there were no monopolistic exploitation. The only important exception to this used to be the claim of the workers to the " full produce of their labour ", to which so much of socialist doctrine traces back. But there are few socialists to-day who believe that in a socialist society the output of each industry would be entirely shared by the workers of that industry ; for this would mean that workers in industries using a great deal of capital would have a much larger income than those in industries using little capital, which most socialists would regard as very unjust. And it is now fairly generally agreed that this particular claim was based on an erroneous interpretation of the facts. But once the claim of the individual worker to the whole of " his " product is disallowed, and the whole of the return from capital is to be divided among all workers, the problem of how to divide it raises the same basic issue.

What the " just price " of a particular commodity or the " fair " remuneration for a particular service is, might conceivably be determined objectively if the quantities needed were independently fixed. If these were given irrespective of cost, the planner might try to find what price or wage is necessary to bring forth this supply. But the planner must also decide how much is to be produced of each kind of goods, and in so doing he determines what will be the just price or fair wage to pay. If the planner decides that fewer architects or watch-makers are wanted and that the need can be met by those who are willing to stay in the trade at a lower remuneration, the " fair " wage will be lower. In deciding the relative importance of the different ends, the planner also decides the relative importance of the different groups and persons. As he is not supposed to treat the people merely as a means, he must take account of these effects and consciously balance the importance of the different ends against the effects of his decision. This means, however, that he will necessarily exercise direct control over the conditions of the different people.

This applies to the relative position of individuals no less than to that of the different occupational groups. We are in general far too apt to think of incomes within a given trade or profession as more or less uniform. But the differences between the incomes, not only of the most and the least successful doctor or architect, writer or cinema actor, boxer or jockey, but also of the more and the less successful plumber or market gardener, grocer or tailor, are as great as those between the propertied and the property-less classes. And although, no doubt, there would be some attempt at standardisation by creating categories, the necessity of discrimination between individuals would remain the same, whether it were exercised by fixing their individual incomes or by allocating them to particular categories.

We need say no more about the likelihood of men in a free society submitting to such control—or about their remaining free if they submitted. On the whole question what John Stuart Mill wrote nearly a hundred years ago remains equally true to-day :

> A fixed rule, like that of equality, might be acquiesced in, and so might chance, or an external necessity ; but that a handful of human beings should weigh everybody in the balance, and give more to one and less to another at their sole pleasure and judgement, would not be borne unless from persons believed to be more than men, and backed by supernatural terrors.[1]

* * * * *

These difficulties need not lead to open clashes so long as socialism is merely the aspiration of a limited and fairly homogeneous group. They come to the surface only when a socialist policy is actually attempted with the support of the many different groups which together compose the majority of a people. Then it soon becomes the one burning question which of the different sets of ideals shall be imposed upon all by making the whole resources of the country serve it. It is because successful planning requires the creation of a common view on the essential values that the restriction of our freedom with regard to material things touches so directly on our spiritual freedom.

Socialists, the cultivated parents of the barbarous offspring they have produced, traditionally hope to solve this problem by education. But what does education mean in this respect ? Surely we have learnt that knowledge cannot create new ethical values, that no amount of learning will lead people to hold the same views on the moral issues which a conscious ordering of

[1] J. S. Mill, *Principles of Political Economy*, Bk. I, Ch. II, Para. 4.

all social relations raises. It is not rational conviction but the acceptance of a creed which is required to justify a particular plan. And, indeed, socialists everywhere were the first to recognise that the task they had set themselves required the general acceptance of a common *Weltanschauung*, of a definite set of values. It was in these efforts to produce a mass movement supported by such a single world view, that the socialists first created most of the instruments of indoctrination of which Nazis and Fascists have made such effective use.

In Germany and Italy the Nazis and Fascists did indeed not have much to invent. The usages of the new political movements which pervaded all aspects of life had in both countries already been introduced by the socialists. The idea of a political party which embraces all activities of the individual from the cradle to the grave, which claims to guide his views on everything, and which delights in making all problems questions of party-*Weltanschauung*, was first put into practice by the socialists. An Austrian socialist writer, speaking of the socialist movement of his country, reports with pride that it was its " characteristic feature that it created special organisations for every field of activities of workers and employees ".[1] But though the Austrian socialists may have gone further in this respect than others, the situation was not very different elsewhere. It was not the Fascists but the socialists who began to collect children from the tenderest age into political organisations to make sure that they grew up as good proletarians. It was not the Fascists but the socialists who first thought of organising sports and games, football and hiking, in party clubs where the members would not be infected by other views. It was the socialists who first insisted that the party member should distinguish himself from others by the modes of greeting and the forms of address. It was they who by their organisation of " cells " and devices for the permanent supervision of private life created the prototype of the totalitarian party. *Balilla* and *Hitlerjugend*, *Dopolavoro* and *Kraft durch Freude*, political uniforms and military party formations, are all little more than imitations of older socialist institutions.[2]

* * * * *

So long as the socialist movement in a country is closely bound up with the interests of a particular group, usually the more highly skilled industrial workers, the problem of creating a common view on the desirable status of the different members of society is comparatively simple. The movement is immedi-

[1] G. Wieser, *Ein Staat stirbt, Oesterreich 1934–1938*, Paris, 1938, p. 41.
[2] The political " book clubs " in this country provide a not unimportant parallel.

ately concerned with the status of one particular group and its
aim is to raise that status relatively to other groups. The character of the problem changes, however, as in the course of the
progressive advance towards socialism it becomes more and more
evident to everybody that his income and general position is
determined by the coercive apparatus of the state, that he can
maintain or improve his position only as a member of an organised
group capable of influencing or controlling the state machine
in his interest. In the tug-of-war between the various pressure
groups which arises at this stage, it is by no means necessary
that the interests of the poorest and most numerous groups
should prevail. Nor is it necessarily an advantage for the older
socialist parties, who avowedly represented the interests of a
particular group, to have been the first in the field, and to have
designed their whole ideology to appeal to the manual workers
in industry. Their very success, and their insistence on the
acceptance of the whole creed, is bound to create a powerful
counter-movement—not by the capitalists, but by the very
large and equally propertyless classes who find their relative
status threatened by the advance of the élite of the industrial
workers.

Socialist theory and socialist tactics, even where they have not
been dominated by Marxist dogma, have been based everywhere
on the idea of a division of society into two classes with common
but mutually conflicting interests : capitalists and industrial
workers. Socialism counted on a rapid disappearance of the
old middle class and completely disregarded the rise of a new
middle class, the countless army of clerks and typists, adminis-
trative workers and school teachers, tradesmen and small officials,
and the lower ranks of the professions. For a time these classes
often provided many of the leaders of the labour movement.
But as it became increasingly clear that the position of those
classes was deteriorating relatively to that of the industrial workers,
the ideals which guided the latter lost much of their appeal to
the others. While they were all socialists in the sense that they
disliked the capitalist system and wanted a deliberate sharing
out of wealth according to their ideas of justice, these ideas
proved to be very different from those embodied in the practice
of the older socialist parties.

The means which the old socialist parties had successfully
employed to secure the support of one occupational group—the
raising of their relative economic position—cannot be used to
secure the support of all. There are bound to arise rival socialist
movements that appeal to the support of those whose relative
position is worsened. There is a great deal of truth in the
often heard statement that Fascism and National Socialism are

a sort of middle-class socialism—only that in Italy and Germany the supporters of these new movements were economically hardly a middle class any longer. It was to a large extent a revolt of a new under-privileged class against the labour aristocracy which the industrial labour movement had created. There can be little doubt that no single economic factor has contributed more to help these movements than the envy of the unsuccessful professional man, the university trained engineer or lawyer, and of the " white collared proletariat " in general, of the engine driver or compositor and other members of the strongest trade unions whose income was many times theirs. Nor can there be much doubt that in terms of money income the average member of the rank and file of the Nazi movement in its early years was poorer than the average trade unionist or member of the older socialist party—a circumstance which only gained poignancy from the fact that the former had often seen better days and were frequently still living in surroundings which were the result of this past. The expression " class struggle *à rebours* ", current in Italy at the time of the rise of Fascism, did point to a very important aspect of the movement. The conflict between the Fascist or National-Socialist and the older socialist parties must indeed very largely be regarded as the kind of conflict which is bound to arise between rival socialist factions. There was no difference between them about the question of it being the will of the state which should assign to each person his proper place in society. But there were, as there always will be, most profound differences about what are the proper places of the different classes and groups.

* * * * *

The old socialist leaders, who had always regarded their parties as the natural spearhead of the future general movement towards socialism, found it difficult to understand that with every extension in the use of socialist methods the resentment of large poor classes should turn against them. But while the old socialist parties, or the organised labour in particular industries, had usually not found it unduly difficult to come to an understanding for joint action with the employers in their particular industries, very large classes were left out in the cold. To them, and not without some justification, the more prosperous sections of the labour movement seemed to belong to the exploiting rather than to the exploited class.[1]

[1] It is now twelve years since one of the leading European socialist intellectuals, Hendrick de Man (who has since consistently developed further and made his peace with the Nazis), observed that " for the first time since the beginning of socialism, anti-capitalist resentments are turning against the socialist movement " (*Sozialismus und National-Faszismus*, Potsdam, 1931, p. 6).

The resentment of the lower middle class, from which Fascism and National Socialism recruited so large a proportion of their supporters, was intensified by the fact that their education and training had in many instances made them aspire to directing positions, and that they regarded themselves as entitled to be members of the directing class. While the younger generation, out of that contempt for profit-making fostered by socialist teaching, spurned independent positions which involved risk, and flocked in ever-increasing numbers into salaried positions which promised security, they demanded a place yielding them the income and power to which in their opinion their training entitled them. While they believed in an organised society, they expected a place in that society very different from that which society ruled by labour seemed to offer. They were quite ready to take over the methods of the older socialism but intended to employ them in the service of a different class. The movement was able to attract all those who, while they agreed on the desirability of the state controlling all economic activity, disagreed with the ends for which the aristocracy of the industrial workers used their political strength.

The new socialist movement started with several tactical advantages. Labour socialism had grown in a democratic and liberal world, adapting its tactics to it and taking over many of the ideals of liberalism. Its protagonists still believed that the creation of socialism as such would solve all problems. Fascism and National-Socialism, on the other hand, grew out of the experience of an increasingly regulated society awakening to the fact that democratic and international socialism was aiming at incompatible ideals. Their tactics were developed in a world already dominated by socialist policy and the problems it creates. They had no illusions about the possibility of a democratic solution of problems which require more agreement among people than can reasonably be expected. They had no illusions about the capacity of reason to decide all the questions of the relative importance of the wants of different men or groups which planning inevitably raises, or about the formula of equality providing an answer. They knew that the strongest group which rallied enough supporters in favour of a new hierarchical order of society, and which frankly promised privileges to the classes to which it appealed, was likely to obtain the support of all those who were disappointed because they had been promised equality but found that they had merely furthered the interest of a particular class. Above all they were successful because they offered a theory, or *Weltanschauung*, which seemed to justify the privileges they promised to their supporters.

CHAPTER IX

SECURITY AND FREEDOM

The whole of society will have become a single office and a single factory with equality of work and equality of pay.
V. I. Lenin, 1917.

In a country where the sole employer is the State, opposition means death by slow starvation. The old principle : who does not work shall not eat, has been replaced by a new one : who does not obey shall not eat.
L. Trotsky, 1937.

LIKE the spurious " economic freedom ", and with more justice, economic security is often represented as an indispensable condition of real liberty. In a sense this is both true and important. Independence of mind or strength of character are rarely found among those who cannot be confident that they will make their way by their own effort. Yet the idea of economic security is no less vague and ambiguous than most other terms in this field ; and because of this the general approval given to the demand for security may become a danger to liberty. Indeed, when security is understood in too absolute a sense, the general striving for it, far from increasing the chances of freedom, becomes the gravest threat to it.

It will be well to contrast at the outset the two kinds of security : the limited one, which can be achieved for all, and which is therefore no privilege but a legitimate object of desire ; and the absolute security which in a free society cannot be achieved for all and which ought not to be given as a privilege—except in a few special instances such as that of the judges, where complete independence is of paramount importance. These two kinds of security are, first, security against severe physical privation, the certainty of a given minimum of sustenance for all ; and, secondly, the security of a given standard of life, or of the relative position which one person or group enjoys compared with others ; or, as we may put it briefly, the security of a minimum income and the security of the particular income a person is thought to deserve. We shall presently see that this distinction largely coincides with the distinction between the security which can be provided for all outside of and supplementary to the market system, and the security which can be provided only for some and only by controlling or abolishing the market.

There is no reason why in a society that has reached the general level of wealth which ours has attained, the first kind of security should not be guaranteed to all without endangering general freedom.   There are difficult questions about the precise standard which should thus be assured; there is particularly the important question whether those who thus rely on the community should indefinitely enjoy all the same liberties as the rest.[1]   An incautious handling of these questions might well cause serious and perhaps even dangerous political problems ; but there can be no doubt that some minimum of food, shelter, and clothing, sufficient to preserve health and the capacity to work, can be assured to everybody.   Indeed, for a considerable part of the population of this country this sort of security has long been achieved.

Nor is there any reason why the state should not assist the individuals in providing for those common hazards of life against which, because of their uncertainty, few individuals can make adequate provision.   Where, as in the case of sickness and accident, neither the desire to avoid such calamities nor the efforts to overcome their consequences are as a rule weakened by the provision of assistance, where, in short, we deal with genuinely insurable risks, the case for the state helping to organise a comprehensive system of social insurance is very strong.   There are many points of detail where those wishing to preserve the competitive system and those wishing to supersede it by something different will disagree on the details of such schemes ; and it is possible under the name of social insurance to introduce measures which tend to make competition more or less ineffective.   But there is no incompatibility in principle between the state providing greater security in this way and the preservation of individual freedom.   To the same category belongs also the increase of security through the state rendering assistance to the victims of such " acts of God " as earthquakes and floods.   Wherever communal action can mitigate disasters against which the individual can neither attempt to guard himself, nor make provision for the consequences, such communal action should undoubtedly be taken.

There is, finally, the supremely important problem of combating general fluctuations of economic activity and the recurrent waves of large-scale unemployment which accompany them.   This is, of course, one of the gravest and most pressing problems of our time.   But, though its solution will require much planning in the good sense, it does not—or at least need not—require that special kind of planning which according to its advocates is to replace the market.   Many economists hope indeed that the ultimate

---

[1] There are also serious problems of international relations which arise if mere citizenship of a country confers the right to a standard of living higher than elsewhere, and which ought not to be dismissed too lightly.

remedy may be found in the field of monetary policy, which would involve nothing incompatible even with nineteenth-century liberalism. Others, it is true, believe that real success can be expected only from the skilful timing of public works undertaken on a very large scale. This might lead to much more serious restrictions of the competitive sphere, and in experimenting in this direction we shall have carefully to watch our step if we are to avoid making all economic activity progressively more dependent on the direction and volume of government expenditure. But this is neither the only, nor, in my opinion, the most promising way of meeting the gravest threat to economic security. In any case, the very necessary efforts to secure protection against these fluctuations do not lead to the kind of planning which constitutes such a threat to our freedom.

*   *   *   *   *

The planning for security which has such an insidious effect on liberty is that for security of a different kind. It is planning designed to protect individuals or groups against diminutions of their income which although in no way deserved yet in a competitive society occur daily, against losses imposing severe hardships having no moral justification yet inseparable from the competitive system. This demand for security is thus another form of the demand for a just remuneration, a remuneration commensurate with the subjective merits and not with the objective results of a man's efforts. This kind of security or justice seems irreconcilable with freedom to choose one's employment.

In any system which for the distribution of men between the different trades and occupations relies on their own choice it is necessary that the remuneration in these trades should correspond to their usefulness to the other members of society, even if this should stand in no relation to subjective merit. Although the results achieved will often be commensurate with efforts and intentions, this cannot always be true in any form of society. It will particularly not be true in the many instances where the usefulness of some trade or special skill is changed by circumstances which could not be foreseen. We all know the tragic plight of the highly trained man whose hard-learned skill has suddenly lost its value because of some invention which greatly benefits the rest of society. The history of the last hundred years is full of instances of this kind, some of them affecting hundreds of thousands of people at a time.

That anybody should suffer a great diminution of his income and bitter disappointment of all his hopes through no fault of his own, and despite hard work and exceptional skill, undoubtedly

offends our sense of justice. The demands of those who suffer
in this way, for state interference on their behalf to safeguard
their legitimate expectations, are certain to receive popular
sympathy and support. The general approval of these demands
has had the effect that governments everywhere have taken
action, not merely to protect the people so threatened from
severe hardship and privation, but to secure to them the continued receipt of their former income and to shelter them from
the vicissitudes of the market.[1]

Certainty of a given income can, however, not be given to all
if any freedom in the choice of one's occupation is to be allowed.
And if it is provided for some it becomes a privilege at the expense
of others whose security is thereby necessarily diminished. That
security of an invariable income can be provided for all only by
the abolition of all freedom in the choice of one's employment is
easily shown. Yet, although such a general guarantee of legitimate expectation is often regarded as the ideal to be aimed at,
it is not a thing which is seriously attempted. What is constantly
being done is to grant this kind of security piecemeal, to this group
and to that, with the result that for those who are left out in the
cold the insecurity constantly increases. No wonder that in
consequence the value attached to the privilege of security
constantly increases, the demand for it becomes more and more
urgent, till in the end no price, not even that of liberty, appears
too high.

*   *   *   *   *

If those whose usefulness is reduced by circumstances which
they could neither foresee nor control were to be protected against
undeserved loss, and those whose usefulness has been increased
in the same way were prevented from making an unmerited gain,
remuneration would soon cease to have any relation to actual
usefulness. It would depend on the views held by some authority
about what a person ought to have done, what he ought to have
foreseen, and how good or bad his intentions were. Such decisions
could not but be to a large extent arbitrary. The application of
this principle would necessarily bring it about that people doing
the same work would receive different remuneration. The
differences in remuneration would then no longer present an
adequate inducement to people to make the changes which are
socially desirable and it would not even be possible for the
individuals affected to judge whether a particular change is
worth the trouble it causes.

[1] Very interesting suggestions of how these hardships might be mitigated within a liberal society, have recently been put forward by Professor W. H. Hutt
in a book which will repay careful study (*Plan for Reconstruction*, 1943).

But if the changes in the distribution of men between different employments, which are constantly necessary in any society, can no longer be brought about by pecuniary " rewards " and " penalties " (which have no necessary connection with subjective merit), they must be brought about by direct orders. When a person's income is guaranteed he can neither be allowed to stay in his job merely because he likes it, nor to choose what other work he would like to do. As it is not he who makes the gain or suffers the loss dependent on his moving or not moving, the choice must be made for him by those who control the distribution of the available income.

The problem of the adequate incentives which arises here is commonly discussed as if it were a problem mainly of the willingness of people to do their best. But this, although important, is not the whole, nor even the most important, aspect of the problem. It is not merely that if we want people to give their best we must make it worth while for them. What is more important is that if we want to leave them the choice, if they are to be able to judge what they ought to do, they must be given some readily intelligible yardstick by which to measure the social importance of the different occupations. Even with the best will in the world it would be impossible for anyone intelligently to choose between various alternatives if the advantages they offered him stood in no relation to their usefulness to society. To know whether as the result of a change a man ought to leave a trade and an environment which he has come to like, and exchange it for another, it is necessary that the changed relative value of these occupations to society should find expression in the remunerations they offer.

The problem is, of course, even more important because in the world as it is men are, in fact, not likely to give their best for long periods unless their own interests are directly involved. At least for great numbers some external pressure is needed if they are to give their best. The problem of incentives in this sense is a very real one, both in the sphere of ordinary labour and in those of the managerial activities. The application of the engineering technique to a whole nation—and this is what planning means—" raises problems of discipline which are hard to solve ", as has been well described by an American engineer with great experience in government planning, who has clearly seen the problem.

In order to do an engineering job, [he explains], there ought to be surrounding the work a comparatively large area of unplanned economic action. There should be a place from which workers can be drawn, and when a worker is fired he should vanish from the job and from the pay-roll. In the absence of such a free reservoir discipline cannot be maintained without corporal punishment, as with slave labour.[1]

In the sphere of executive work the problem of sanctions for negligence arises in a different but no less serious form. It has been well said that while the last resort of a competitive economy is the bailiff, the ultimate sanction of a planned economy is the hangman.[2] The powers the manager of any plant will have to be given will still be considerable. But no more than in the case of the worker can the manager's position and income in a planned system be made to depend merely on the success or failure of the work under his direction. As neither the risk nor the gain is his, it cannot be his personal judgment, but whether he does what he ought to have done according to some established rule, which must decide. A mistake he " ought " to have avoided is not his own affair, it is a crime against the community and must be treated as such. While so long as he keeps to the safe path of objectively ascertainable duty he may be surer of his income than the capitalist entrepreneur, the danger which threatens him in case of real failure is worse than bankruptcy. He may be economically secure so long as he satisfies his superiors, but this security is bought at the price of the safety of freedom and life.

The conflict with which we have to deal is indeed a quite fundamental one between two irreconcilable types of social organisation, which, from the most characteristic forms in which they appear, have often been described as the commercial and the military type of society. The terms were, perhaps, unfortunate, because they direct attention to unessentials and make it difficult to see that we face here a real alternative and that there is no third possibility. Either both the choice and the risk rest with the individual or he is relieved of both. The army does indeed in many ways represent the closest approach familiar to us to the second type of organisation, where work and worker alike are allotted by authority and where, if the available means are scanty, everybody is alike put on short commons. This is the only system in which the individual can be conceded full economic security and through the extension of which to the whole of society it can be achieved for all its members. This security is, however, inseparable from the restrictions on liberty and the hierarchical order of military life—it is the security of the barracks.

It is possible, of course, to organise sections of an otherwise free society on this principle and there is no reason why this form of life, with its necessary restrictions on individual liberty, should not be open to those who prefer it. Indeed, some voluntary

---

[1] D. C. Coyle, " The Twilight of National Planning," *Harpers' Magazine*, October 1935, p. 558.

[2] W. Roepke, *Die Gesellschaftskrisis der Gegenwart*, Zurich, 1942, p. 172.

labour service on military lines might well be the best form for
the state to provide the certainty of an opportunity for work and
a minimum income for all.   That proposals of this sort have in
the past proved so little acceptable is due to the fact that those
who are willing to surrender their freedom for security have
always demanded that if they give up their full freedom it should
also be taken from those not prepared to do so.   For this claim
it is difficult to find a justification.

The military type of organisation as we know it gives us, however, only a very inadequate picture of what it would be like if
it were extended to the whole of society.   So long as only a part
of society is organised on military lines, the unfreedom of the
members of the military organisation is mitigated by the fact that
there is still a free sphere to which they can move if the restrictions
become too irksome.   If we want to form a picture of what society
would be like if, according to the ideal which has seduced so
many socialists, it was organised as a single great factory, we have
to look to ancient Sparta, or to contemporary Germany, which
after moving for two or three generations in this direction, has
now so nearly reached it.

*   *   *   *   *

In a society used to freedom it is unlikely that many people
would be ready deliberately to purchase security at this price.
But the policies which are now followed everywhere, which hand
out the privilege of security, now to this group and now to that,
are nevertheless rapidly creating conditions in which the striving
for security tends to become stronger than the love of freedom.
The reason for this is that with every grant of complete security
to one group the insecurity of the rest necessarily increases.   If
you guarantee to some a fixed part of a variable cake, the share
left to the rest is bound to fluctuate proportionally more than the
size of the whole.   And the essential element of security which
the competitive system offers, the great variety of opportunities,
is more and more reduced.

Within the market system, security can be granted to particular
groups only by the kind of planning known as restrictionism
(which includes, however, almost all the planning which is actually
practised !).   " Control ", i.e. limitation of output so that prices
will secure an " adequate " return, is the only way in which in
a market economy producers can be guaranteed a certain income.
But this necessarily involves a reduction of opportunities open
to others.   If the producer, be he entrepreneur or worker, is to
be protected against underbidding by outsiders, it means that
others who are worse off are precluded from sharing in the relatively greater prosperity of the controlled industries.   Every

restriction on the freedom of entry into a trade reduces the security of all those outside it. And as the number of those whose income is secured in this manner increases, the field of alternative opportunities is restricted which are open to anyone who suffers a loss of income ; and for those unfavourably affected by any change the chance of avoiding a fatal diminution of their income is correspondingly diminished. And if, as has become increasingly true, in each trade in which conditions improve, the members are allowed to exclude others in order to secure to themselves the full gain in the form of higher wages or profits, those in the trades where demand has fallen have nowhere to go and every change becomes the cause of large unemployment. There can be little doubt that it is largely a consequence of the striving for security by these means in the last decades that unemployment and thus insecurity for large sections of the population has so much increased.

In this country such restrictions, especially those affecting the intermediate strata of society, have assumed important dimensions only in comparatively recent times, and we have scarcely yet realised their full consequences. The utter hopelessness of the position of those who, in a society which has thus grown rigid, are left outside the range of sheltered occupation, and the magnitude of the gulf which separates them from the fortunate possessor of jobs for whom protection against competition has made it unnecessary to budge ever so little to make room for those without can only be appreciated by those who have experienced it. It is not a question of the fortunate ones giving up their places, but merely that they should share in the common misfortune by some reduction of their incomes, or frequently even merely by some sacrifice of their prospects of improvement. The protection of their " standard of life ", of the " fair price ", or the " professional income " to which they regard themselves as entitled, and in the protection of which they receive the support of the state, precludes this. In consequence, instead of prices, wages, and individual incomes, it is now employment and production which have become subject to violent fluctuations. There has never been a worse and more cruel exploitation of one class by another than that of the weaker or less fortunate members of a group of producers by the well-established which has been made possible by the " regulation " of competition. Few catchwords have done so much harm as the ideal of a " stabilisation " of particular prices (or wages) which, while securing the income of some, makes the position of the rest more and more precarious.

Thus, the more we try to provide full security by interfering with the market system, the greater the insecurity becomes ; and, what is worse, the greater becomes the contrast between the security of those to whom it is granted as a privilege and the ever-increasing insecurity of the under-privileged. And the more security becomes a privilege, and the greater the danger to those excluded from it, the higher will security be prized. As the number of the privileged increases and the difference between their security and the insecurity of the others increases, a completely new set of social values gradually arises. It is no longer independence but security which gives rank and status, the certain right to a pension more than confidence in his making good which makes a young man eligible for marriage, while insecurity becomes the dreaded state of the pariah in which those who in their youth have been refused admission to the haven of a salaried position remain for life.

* * * * *

The general endeavour to achieve security by restrictive measures, tolerated or supported by the state, has in the course of time produced a progressive transformation of society—a transformation in which, as in so many other ways, Germany has led and the other countries have followed. This development has been hastened by another effect of socialist teaching, the deliberate disparagement of all activities involving economic risk and the moral opprobrium cast on the gains which make risks worth taking but which only few can win. We cannot blame our young men when they prefer the safe, salaried position to the risk of enterprise after they have heard from their earliest youth the former described as the superior, more unselfish and disinterested occupation. The younger generation of to-day has grown up in a world in which in school and press the spirit of commercial enterprise has been represented as disreputable and the making of profit as immoral, where to employ a hundred people is represented as exploitation but to command the same number as honourable. Older people may regard this as an exaggeration of the present state of affairs, but the daily experience of the University teacher leaves little doubt that as a result of anti-capitalist propaganda values have already altered far in advance of the change in institutions which has yet taken place in this country. The question is whether by changing our institutions to satisfy the new demands, we shall not unwittingly destroy values which we still rate higher.

The change in the structure of society involved in the victory of the ideal of security over that of independence cannot be better illustrated than by a comparison of what ten or twenty years ago could still be regarded as the English and the German type of society. However great the influence of the army may have been in the latter country, it is a grave mistake to ascribe what the Englishman regarded as the " military " character of German society mainly to that influence. The difference went much deeper than could be explained on that ground, and the peculiar attributes of German society existed no less in circles in which the properly military influence was negligible than in those in which it was strong. It was not so much that at almost all times a larger part of the German people was organised for war than was true in other countries, but that the same type of organisation was employed for so many other purposes, which gave German society its peculiar character. It was that a larger part of the civil life of Germany than of any other country was deliberately organised from the top, that so large a proportion of her people did not regard themselves as independent but as appointed functionaries, which gave her social structure its peculiar character. Germany had, as the Germans themselves boasted, for long been a *Beamtenstaat* in which not only in the Civil Service proper but in almost all spheres of life income and status were assigned and guaranteed by some authority.

While it is doubtful whether the spirit of freedom can anywhere be extirpated by force, it is not certain that any people would successfully withstand the process by which it was slowly smothered in Germany. Where distinction and rank is achieved almost exclusively by becoming a salaried servant of the state, where to do one's assigned duty is regarded as more laudable than to choose one's own field of usefulness, where all pursuits that do not give a recognised place in the official hierarchy or a claim to a fixed income are regarded as inferior and even somewhat disreputable, it is too much to expect that many will long prefer freedom to security. And where the alternative to security in a dependent position is a most precarious position, in which one is despised alike for success and for failure, only few will resist the temptation of safety at the price of freedom. Once things have gone so far, liberty indeed becomes almost a mockery, since it can be purchased only by the sacrifice of most of the good things of this earth. In this state it is little surprising that more and more people should come to feel that without economic security liberty is " not worth having " and that they are willing to sacrifice their liberty for security. But it is disquieting to find Professor Harold Laski in this country employing the very same argument which has perhaps done more than any other to induce the German people to sacrifice their liberty.[1]

There can be no question that adequate security against severe

[1] H. J. Laski, *Liberty in the Modern State* (Pelican edition 1937, p. 51) : " Those who know the normal life of the poor, its haunting sense of impending disaster, its fitful search for beauty which perpetually eludes, will realise well enough that, without economic security, liberty is not worth having."

privation, and the reduction of the avoidable causes of misdirected effort and consequent disappointment, will have to be one of the main goals of policy. But if these endeavours are to be successful and not to destroy individual freedom, security must be provided outside the market and competition be left to function unobstructed. Some security is essential if freedom is to be preserved, because most men are willing to bear the risk which freedom inevitably involves only so long as that risk is not too great. But while this is a truth of which we must never lose sight, nothing is more fatal than the present fashion among intellectual leaders of extolling security at the expense of freedom. It is essential that we should re-learn frankly to face the fact that freedom can only be had at a price and that as individuals we must be prepared to make severe material sacrifices to preserve our liberty. If we want to retain this we must regain the conviction on which the rule of liberty in the Anglo-Saxon countries has been based and which Benjamin Franklin expressed in a phrase applicable to us in our lives as individuals no less than as nations: "Those who would give up essential liberty to purchase a little temporary safety deserve neither liberty nor safety."

CHAPTER X

WHY THE WORST GET ON TOP

All power corrupts, absolute power corrupts absolutely.
Lord Acton.

WE must now examine a belief from which many who regard the advent of totalitarianism as inevitable derive consolation and which seriously weakens the resistance of many others who would oppose it with all their might if they fully apprehended its nature. It is the belief that the most repellent features of the totalitarian regimes are due to the historical accident that they were established by groups of blackguards and thugs. Surely, it is argued, if in Germany the creation of a totalitarian regime brought the Streichers and Killingers, the Leys and Heines, the Himmlers and Heydrichs to power, this may prove the viciousness of the German character, but not that the rise of such people is the necessary consequence of a totalitarian system. Why should it not be possible that the same sort of system, if it be necessary to achieve important ends, be run by decent people for the good of the community as a whole ?

We must not deceive ourselves into believing that all good people must be democrats or will necessarily wish to have a share in the government. Many, no doubt, would rather entrust it to somebody whom they think more competent. Although this might be unwise, there is nothing bad or dishonourable in approving a dictatorship of the good. Totalitarianism, we can already hear it argued, is a powerful system alike for good and evil, and the purpose for which it will be used depends entirely on the dictators. And those who think that it is not the system which we need fear, but the danger that it might be run by bad men, might even be tempted to forestal this danger by seeing that it is established in time by good men.

No doubt an English " fascist " system would greatly differ from the Italian or German models ; no doubt if the transition were effected without violence, we might expect to get a better type of leader. And if I had to live under a fascist system I have no doubt that I would rather live under one run by Englishmen than under one run by anybody else. Yet all this does not mean that, judged on our present standards, a British fascist system would in the end prove so very different or much less intolerable than its prototypes. There are strong reasons for believing that what to us appear the worst features of the existing totalitarian systems are not accidental by-products, but phenomena which totalitarianism is certain sooner or later to produce. Just as the democratic statesman who sets out to plan economic life will soon be confronted with the alternative of either assuming dictatorial powers or abandoning his plans, so the totalitarian dictator would soon have to choose between disregard of ordinary morals and failure. It is for this reason that the unscrupulous and uninhibited are likely to be more successful in a society tending towards totalitarianism. Who does not see this has not yet grasped the full width of the gulf which separates totalitarianism from a liberal regime, the utter difference between the whole moral atmosphere under collectivism and the essentially individualist Western civilisation.

The " moral basis of collectivism " has, of course, been much debated in the past ; but what concerns us here is not its moral basis but its moral results. The usual discussions of the ethical aspects of collectivism refer to the question whether collectivism is demanded by existing moral convictions ; or what moral convictions would be required if collectivism is to produce the hoped-for results. Our question, however, is what moral views will be produced by a collectivist organisation of society, or what views are likely to rule it. The interaction between morals and institutions may well have the effect that the ethics produced by collectivism will be altogether different from the moral ideals that lead to the demand for collectivism. While we are apt to think that, since the desire for a collectivist system springs from high moral motives, such a system must be the breeding ground for the highest virtues, there is, in fact, no reason why any system should necessarily enhance those attitudes which serve the purpose for which it was designed. The ruling moral views will depend partly on the qualities that will lead individuals to success in a collectivist or totalitarian system, and partly on the requirements of the totalitarian machinery.

*   *   *   *   *

We must here return for a moment to the position which precedes the suppression of democratic institutions and the creation of a totalitarian regime. In this stage it is the general demand for quick and determined government action that is the dominating element in the situation, dissatisfaction with the slow and cumbersome course of democratic procedure which makes action for action's sake the goal. It is then the man or the party who seems strong and resolute enough " to get things done " who exercises the greatest appeal. " Strong " in this sense means not merely a numerical majority—it is the ineffectiveness of parliamentary majorities with which people are dissatisfied. What they will seek is somebody with such solid support as to inspire confidence that he can carry out whatever he wants. It is here that the new type of party, organised on military lines, comes in.

In the Central European countries the socialist parties had familiarised the masses with political organisations of a semi-military character designed to absorb as much as possible of the private life of the members. All that was wanted to give one group overwhelming power was to carry the same principle somewhat further, to seek strength not in the assured votes of huge numbers at occasional elections, but in the absolute and unreserved support of a smaller but more thoroughly organised body. The chance of imposing a totalitarian regime on a whole people depends on the leader first collecting round him a group which is prepared voluntarily to submit to that totalitarian discipline which they are to impose by force upon the rest.

Although the socialist parties had the strength to get anything if they had cared to use force, they were reluctant to do so. They had, without knowing it, set themselves a task which only the ruthless, ready to disregard the barriers of accepted morals, can execute.

That socialism can be put into practice only by methods which most socialists disapprove is, of course, a lesson learnt by many social reformers in the past. The old socialist parties were inhibited by their democratic ideals, they did not possess the ruthlessness required for the performance of their chosen task. It is characteristic that both in Germany and Italy the success of Fascism was preceded by the refusal of the socialist parties to take over the responsibilities of government. They were unwilling wholeheartedly to employ the methods to which they had pointed the way. They still hoped for the miracle of a majority agreeing on a particular plan for the organisation of the whole of society; others had already learnt the lesson that in a planned society the question can no longer be on what a majority of the people agree, but what is the largest single group whose members agree sufficiently to make unified direction of all affairs possible; or, if no such group large enough to enforce its views exists, how it can be created and who will succeed in creating it.

There are three main reasons why such a numerous and strong group with fairly homogeneous views is not likely to be formed by the best but rather by the worst elements of any society. By our standards the principles on which such a group would be selected will be almost entirely negative.

In the first instance, it is probably true that in general the higher the education and intelligence of individuals becomes, the more their views and tastes are differentiated and the less likely they are to agree on a particular hierarchy of values. It is a corollary of this that if we wish to find a high degree of uniformity and similarity of outlook, we have to descend to the regions of lower moral and intellectual standards where the more primitive and " common " instincts and tastes prevail. This does not mean that the majority of people have low moral standards ; it merely means that the largest group of people whose values are very similar are the people with low standards. It is, as it were, the lowest common denominator which unites the largest number of people. If a numerous group is needed, strong enough to impose their views on the values of life on all the rest, it will never be those with highly differentiated and developed tastes—it will be those who form the " mass " in the derogatory sense of the term, the least original and independent, who will be able to put the weight of their numbers behind their particular ideals.

If, however, a potential dictator had to rely entirely on those whose uncomplicated and primitive instincts happen to be very similar, their number would scarcely give sufficient weight to their endeavours. He will have to increase their numbers by converting more to the same simple creed.

Here comes in the second negative principle of selection : he will be able to obtain the support of all the docile and gullible, who have no strong convictions of their own but are prepared to accept a ready-made system of values if it is only drummed into their ears sufficiently loudly and frequently. It will be those whose vague and imperfectly formed ideas are easily swayed and whose passions and emotions are readily aroused who will thus swell the ranks of the totalitarian party.

It is in connection with the deliberate effort of the skilful demagogue to weld together a closely coherent and homogeneous body of supporters that the third and perhaps most important negative element of selection enters. It seems to be almost a law of human nature that it is easier for people to agree on a negative programme, on the hatred of an enemy, on the envy of those better off, than on any positive task. The contrast between the " we " and the " they ", the common fight against those outside the group, seems to be an essential ingredient in any creed which will solidly knit together a group for common action. It is consequently always employed by those who seek, not merely support of a policy, but the unreserved allegiance of huge masses. From their point of view it has the great advantage of leaving them greater freedom of action than almost any positive programme. The enemy, whether he be internal like the " Jew " or the " Kulak ", or external, seems to be an indispensable requisite in the armoury of a totalitarian leader.

That in Germany it was the Jew who became the enemy till his place was taken by the " plutocracies " was no less a result of the anti-capitalist resentment on which the whole movement was based than the selection of the Kulak in Russia. In Germany and Austria the Jew had come to be regarded as the representative of capitalism because a traditional dislike of large classes of the population for commercial pursuits had left these more readily accessible to a group that was practically excluded from the more highly esteemed occupations. It is the old story of the alien race being admitted only to the less respected trades and then being hated still more for practising them. The fact that German anti-semitism and anti-capitalism spring from the same root is of great importance for the understanding of what has happened there, but this is rarely grasped by foreign observers.

*   *   *   *   *

To treat the universal tendency of collectivist policy to become nationalistic as due entirely to the necessity for securing unhesitating support would be to neglect another and no less important factor. It may indeed be questioned whether anybody can realistically conceive of a collectivist programme other than in the service of a limited group, whether collectivism can exist in any other form than that of some kind of particularism, be it nationalism, racialism, or class-ism. The belief in the community of aims and interests with fellow-men seems to presuppose a greater degree of similarity of outlook and thought than exists between men merely as human beings. If the other members of one's group cannot all be personally known, they must at least be of the same kind as those around us, think and talk in the same way and about the same kind of things, in order that we may identify ourselves with them. Collectivism on a world scale seems to be unthinkable—except in the service of a small ruling élite. It would certainly raise not only technical but above all moral problems which none of our socialists are willing to face. If the English proletarian is entitled to an equal share of the income now derived from England's capital resources, and of the control of their use, because they are the result of exploitation, so on the same principle all the Indians would be entitled not only to the income from but also to the use of a proportional share of the British capital. But what socialists seriously contemplate the equal division of existing capital resources among the people of the world ? They all regard the capital as belonging not to humanity but to the nation—though even within the nation few would dare to advocate that the richer regions should be deprived of some of " their " capital equipment in order to help the poorer regions. What socialists proclaim as a duty towards the fellow members of the existing states, they are not prepared to grant to the foreigner. From a consistent collectivist point of view the claims of the " Have-Not " nations for a new division of the world are entirely justified—though, if consistently applied, those who demand it most loudly would lose by it almost as much as the richest nations. They are, therefore, careful not to base their claims on any equalitarian principles but on their pretended superior capacity to organise other peoples.

One of the inherent contradictions of the collectivist philosophy is, that while basing itself on the humanistic morals which individualism has developed, it is practicable only within a relatively small group. That socialism so long as it remains theoretical, is internationalist, while as soon as it is put into practice, whether in Russia or in Germany, it becomes violently nationalist, is one of the reasons why " liberal socialism " as most people in the Western world imagine it is purely theoretical, while the practice of socialism is everywhere totalitarian.[1] Collectivism has no room for the wide humanitarianism of liberalism but only for the narrow particularism of the totalitarian.

If the " community " or the state are prior to the individual, if they have ends of their own independent of and superior to those of the individuals, only those individuals who work for the same ends can be regarded as members of the community. It is a necessary consequence of this view that a person is respected only as a member of the group, that is, only if and in so far as he works for the recognised common ends, and that he derives his whole dignity only from this membership and not merely from being man. Indeed, the very concepts of humanity and therefore of any form of internationalism are entirely products of the individualist view of man, and there can be no place for them in a collectivist system of thought.[2]

Apart from the basic fact that the community of collectivism can extend only as far as the unity of purpose of the individuals exists or can be created, several contributory factors strengthen the tendency of collectivism to become particularist and exclusive. Of these one of the most important is that the desire of the individual to identify himself with a group is very frequently the result of a feeling of inferiority, and that therefore his want will only be satisfied if membership of the group confers some superiority over outsiders. Sometimes, it seems, the very fact that these violent instincts which the individual knows he must

---

[1] Cf. now the instructive discussion in F. Borkenau, *Socialism, National or International ?*, 1942.

[2] It is entirely in the spirit of collectivism when Nietzsche makes his Zarathustra say :

" A thousand goals have existed hitherto, for a thousand people existed. But the fetter for the thousand necks is still lacking, the one goal is still lacking. Humanity has no goal yet.

" But tell me, I pray, my brethren : if the goal be lacking to humanity, is not humanity itself lacking ? "

curb within the group can be given a free range in the collective action towards the outsider, becomes a further inducement for merging personality in that of the group. There is a profound truth expressed in the title of R. Niebuhr's *Moral Man and Immoral Society*—however little we can follow him in the conclusions he draws from his thesis. There is indeed, as he says elsewhere, " an increasing tendency among modern men to imagine themselves ethical because they have delegated their vices to larger and larger groups." [1] To act on behalf of a group seems to free people of many of the moral restraints which control their behaviour as individuals within the group.

The definitely antagonistic attitude which most planners take towards internationalism is further explained by the fact that in the existing world all outside contacts of a group are obstacles to their effectively planning the sphere in which they can attempt it. It is therefore no accident that, as the editor of one of the most comprehensive collective studies on planning has discovered to his chagrin, " most ' planners ' are militant nationalists ".[2]

The nationalist and imperialist propensities of socialist planners, much more common than is generally recognised, are not always as flagrant as, for example, in the case of the Webbs and some of the other early Fabians, with whom enthusiasm for planning was characteristically combined with the veneration for the large and powerful political units and a contempt for the small state. The historian Elie Halévy, speaking of the Webbs when he first knew them forty years ago, records that

> their socialism was profoundly anti-liberal. They did not hate the Tories, indeed they were extraordinarily lenient to them, but they had no mercy for Gladstonian Liberalism. It was the time of the Boer War and both the advanced liberals and the men who were beginning to form the Labour Party had generously sided with the Boers against British Imperialism, in the name of freedom and humanity. But the two Webbs and their friend, Bernard Shaw, stood apart. They were ostentatiously imperialistic. The independence of small nations might mean something to the liberal individualist. It meant nothing to collectivists like themselves. I can still hear Sidney Webb explaining to me that the future belonged to the great administrative nations, where the officials govern and the police keep order.

And elsewhere Halévy quotes Bernard Shaw arguing, about the same time, that " the world is to the big and powerful states by

---

[1] Quoted from an article of Dr. Niebuhr's by E. H. Carr, *The Twenty Years' Crisis*, 1941, p. 203.

[2] Findlay MacKenzie (ed.), *Planned Society, Yesterday, Today, Tomorrow: A Symposium*, 1937, p. xx.

necessity ; and the little ones must come within their border or be crushed out of existence ".[1]

I have quoted at length these passages, which would not surprise one in a description of the German ancestors of national socialism, because they provide so characteristic an example of that glorification of power which easily leads from socialism to nationalism and which profoundly affects the ethical views of all collectivists. So far as the rights of small nations are concerned, Marx and Engels were little better than most other consistent collectivists, and the views they occasionally expressed about Czechs or Poles resemble those of contemporary National Socialists.[2]

* * * * *

While to the great individualist social philosophers of the nineteenth century, to a Lord Acton or Jacob Burchardt, down to contemporary socialists, like Bertrand Russell, who have inherited the liberal tradition, power itself has always appeared the archevil, to the strict collectivist it is a goal in itself. It is not only, as Russell has so well described, that the desire to organise social life according to a unitary plan itself springs largely from a desire for power.[3] It is even more the outcome of the fact that in order to achieve their end collectivists must create power— power over men wielded by other men—of a magnitude never before known, and that their success will depend on the extent to which they achieve such power.

This remains true even though many liberal socialists are guided in their endeavours by the tragic illusion that by depriving private individuals of the power they possess in an individualist system, and by transferring this power to society, they can thereby extinguish power. What all those who argue in this manner overlook is that by concentrating power so that it can be used in the service of a single plan, it is not merely transferred but infinitely heightened ; that by uniting in the hands of some single body power formerly exercised independently by many, an amount of power is created infinitely greater than any that existed before, so much more far-reaching as almost to be different in kind. It is entirely fallacious when it is sometimes argued that the great power exercised by a Central Planning Board would be " no greater than the power collectively exercised by private boards of directors ".[4] There is, in a competitive society, nobody who

[1] E. Halévy, *L'Ere des Tyrannies*, Paris, 1938, p. 217, and *History of the English People*, Epilogue, vol. I, pp. 105–6.
[2] Cf. K. Marx, *Revolution and Counter-revolution*, and Engels' letter to Marx, May 23, 1851.
[3] Bertrand Russell, *The Scientific Outlook*, 1931, p. 211.
[4] B. E. Lippincott, in his Introduction to O. Lange and F. M. Taylor, *On the Economic Theory of Socialism*, Minneapolis, 1938, p. 35.

can exercise even a fraction of the power which a socialist planning board would possess, and if nobody can consciously use the power, it is just an abuse of words to assert that it rests with all the capitalists put together.[1]   It is merely a play upon words to speak of the " power collectively exercised by private boards of directors " so long as they do not combine to concerted action —which would, of course, mean the end of competition and the creation of a planned economy.   To split or decentralise power is necessarily to reduce the absolute amount of power and the competitive system is the only system designed to minimise by decentralisation the power exercised by man over man.

We have seen before how the separation of economic and political aims is an essential guarantee of individual freedom and how it is consequently attacked by all collectivists.   To this we must now add that the " substitution of political for economic power " now so often demanded means necessarily the substitution of power from which there is no escape for a power which is always limited.   What is called economic power, while it can be an instrument of coercion, is in the hands of private individuals never exclusive or complete power, never power over the whole life of a person.   But centralised as an instrument of political power it creates a degree of dependence scarcely distinguishable from slavery.

*   *   *   *   *

From the two central features of every collectivist system, the need for a commonly accepted system of ends of the group, and the all-overriding desire to give to the group the maximum of power to achieve these ends, grows a definite system of morals, which on some points coincides and on others violently contrasts with ours—but differs from it in one point which makes it doubtful whether we can call it morals : that it does not leave the individual conscience free to apply its own rules and does not even know any general rules which the individual is required or allowed to observe in all circumstances.   This makes collectivist morals so different from what we have known as morals that we find it difficult to discover any principle in them, which they nevertheless possess.

The difference of principle is very much the same as that which we have already considered in connection with the Rule of Law.

---

[1] We must not allow ourselves to be deceived by the fact that the word power, apart from the sense in which it is used with respect to human beings, is also used in an impersonal (or rather anthropomorphic) sense for any determining cause.   Of course there will always be something that determines everything that happens, and in this sense the amount of power existing must always be the same.   But this is not true of the power consciously wielded by human beings.

Like formal law the rules of individualist ethics, however un-
precise they may be in many respects, are general and absolute ;
they prescribe or prohibit a general type of action irrespective of
whether in the particular instance the ultimate purpose is good
or bad.   To cheat or steal, to torture or betray a confidence, is
held to be bad, irrespective of whether or not in the particular
instance any harm follows from it.   Neither the fact that in a
given instance nobody may be the worse for it, nor any high
purpose for which such an act may have been committed, can
alter the fact that it is bad.   Though we may sometimes be forced
to choose between different evils they remain evils.   The principle
that the end justifies the means is in individualist ethics regarded
as the denial of all morals.   In collectivist ethics it becomes
necessarily the supreme rule ;   there is literally nothing which
the consistent collectivist must not be prepared to do if it serves
" the good of the whole ", because the " good of the whole "
is to him the only criterion of what ought to be done.   The
raison d'état, in which collectivist ethics has found its most explicit
formulation, knows no other limit than that set by expediency
—the suitability of the particular act for the end in view.   And
what the *raison d'état* affirms with respect to the relations between
different countries applies equally to the relations between
different individuals within the collectivist state.   There can be
no limit to what its citizen must not be prepared to do, no act
which his conscience must prevent him from committing, if it
is necessary for an end which the community has set itself or which
his superiors order him to achieve.

*   *   *   *   *

The absence of absolute formal rules in collectivist ethics does
not, of course, mean that there are not some useful habits of the
individuals which a collectivist community will encourage, and
others which it will discourage.   Quite the reverse ;   it will
take a much greater interest in the individual's habits of life
than an individualist community.   To be a useful member of a
collectivist society requires very definite qualities which must
be strengthened by constant practice.   The reason why we
designate these qualities as " useful habits " and can hardly
describe them as moral virtues is that the individual could never
be allowed to put these rules above any definite orders, or to let
them become an obstacle to the achievement of any of the particular aims of his community.   They only serve, as it were, to
fill any gaps which direct orders or the designation of particular
aims may leave, but they can never justify a conflict with the
will of the authority.

The differences between the virtues which will continue to be esteemed under a collectivist system and those which will dis-appear is well illustrated by a comparison of the virtues which even their worst enemies admit the Germans, or rather the "typical Prussian", to possess, and those of which they are commonly thought lacking and in which the English people, with some justification, used to pride themselves as excelling. Few people will deny that the Germans on the whole are industrious and disciplined, thorough and energetic to the degree of ruthlessness, conscientious and single-minded in any tasks they undertake, that they possess a strong sense of order, duty, and strict obedience to authority, and that they often show great readiness to make personal sacrifices and great courage in physical danger. All these make the German an efficient instru-ment in carrying out an assigned task, and they have accordingly been carefully nurtured in the old Prussian state and the new Prussian-dominated Reich. What the "typical German" is often thought to lack are the individualist virtues of tolerance and respect for other individuals and their opinions, of independence of mind and that uprightness of character and readiness to defend one's own convictions against a superior which the Germans them-selves, usually conscious that they lack it, call *Zivilcourage*, of consideration for the weak and infirm, and of that healthy contempt and dislike of power which only an old tradition of personal liberty creates. Deficient they seem also in most of those little yet so important qualities which facilitate the intercourse between men in a free society : kindliness and a sense of humour, personal modesty, and respect for the privacy and belief in the good intentions of one's neighbour.

After what we have already said it will not cause surprise that these individualist virtues are at the same time eminently social virtues, virtues which smooth social contacts and which make con-trol from above less necessary and at the same time more difficult. They are virtues which flourish wherever the individualist or commercial type of society has prevailed and which are missing according as the collectivist or military type of society predom-inates—a difference which is, or was, as noticeable between the various regions of Germany as it has now become of the views which rule in Germany and those characteristic of the West. Till recently, at least, in those parts of Germany which have been longest exposed to the civilising forces of commerce, the old commercial towns of the south and west and the Hanse towns, the general moral concepts were probably much more akin to those of the Western people than to those which have now become dominant all over Germany.

It would, however, be highly unjust to regard the masses of the totalitarian people as devoid of moral fervor because they give unstinted support to a system which to us seems a denial of most moral values. For the great majority of them the opposite is probably true : the intensity of the moral emotions behind a movement like that of National-Socialism or communism can probably be compared only to those of the great religious movements of history. Once you admit that the individual is merely a means to serve the ends of the higher entity called society or the nation, most of those features of totalitarian regimes which horrify us follow of necessity. From the collectivist standpoint intolerance and brutal suppression of dissent, the complete disregard of the life and happiness of the individual, are essential and unavoidable consequences of this basic premise, and the collectivist can admit this and at the same time claim that his system is superior to one in which the " selfish " interests of the individual are allowed to obstruct the full realisation of the ends the community pursues. When German philosophers again and again represent the striving for personal happiness as itself immoral and only the fulfilment of an imposed duty as praiseworthy, they are perfectly sincere, however difficult this may be to understand for those who have been brought up in a different tradition.

Where there is one common all-overriding end there is no room for any general morals or rules. To a limited extent we ourselves experience this in wartime. But even war and the greatest peril had led in this country only to a very moderate approach to totalitarianism, very little setting aside of all other values in the service of a single purpose. But where a few specific ends dominate the whole of society, it is inevitable that occasionally cruelty may become a duty, that acts which revolt all our feeling, such as the shooting of hostages or the killing of the old or sick, should be treated as mere matters of expediency, that the compulsory uprooting and transportation of hundreds of thousands should become an instrument of policy approved by almost everybody except the victims, or that suggestions like that of a " conscription of woman for breeding purposes " can be seriously contemplated. There is always in the eyes of the collectivist a greater goal which these acts serve and which to him justifies them because the pursuit of the common end of society can know no limits in any rights or values of any individual.

But while for the mass of the citizens of the totalitarian state it is often unselfish devotion to an ideal, although one that is repellent to us, which makes them approve and even perform such deeds, this cannot be pleaded for those who guide its policy. To be a useful assistant in the running of a totalitarian state it is not enough that a man should be prepared to accept specious

justification of vile deeds, he must himself be prepared actively
to break every moral rule he has ever known if this seems necessary
to achieve the end set for him.   Since it is the supreme leader
who alone determines the ends, his instruments must have no
moral convictions of their own.   They must, above all, be
unreservedly committed to the person of the leader ; but next
to this the most important thing is that they should be completely
unprincipled and literally capable of everything.   They must
have no ideals of their own which they want to realise, no ideas
about right or wrong which might interfere with the intentions
of the leader.   There is thus in the positions of power little to
attract those who hold moral beliefs of the kind which in the
past have guided the European peoples, little which could compensate for the distastefulness of many of the particular tasks,
and little opportunity to gratify any more idealistic desires, to
recompense for the undeniable risk, the sacrifice of most of the
pleasures of private life and of personal independence which the
posts of great responsibility involve.   The only tastes which are
satisfied are the taste for power as such, the pleasure of being
obeyed and of being part of a well-functioning and immensely
powerful machine to which everything else must give way.

Yet while there is little that is likely to induce men who are
good by our standards to aspire to leading positions in the totalitarian machine, and much to deter them, there will be special
opportunities for the ruthless and unscrupulous.   There will be
jobs to be done about the badness of which taken by themselves
nobody has any doubt, but which have to be done in the service
of some higher end, and which have to be executed with the
same expertness and efficiency as any others.   And as there will
be need for actions which are bad in themselves, and which all
those still influenced by traditional morals will be reluctant to
perform, the readiness to do bad things becomes a path to pro-
motion and power.   The positions in a totalitarian society in
which it is necessary to practice cruelty and intimidation, deliberate deception and spying, are numerous.   Neither the Gestapo
nor the administration of a concentration camp, neither the
Ministry of Propaganda nor the SA or SS (or their Italian or
Russian counterparts) are suitable places for the exercise of
humanitarian feelings.   Yet it is through positions like these that
the road to the highest positions in the totalitarian state leads.
It is only too true when a distinguished American economist
concludes from a similar brief enumeration of the duties of the
authorities of a collectivist state that

> they would have to do these things whether they wanted to or not :
> and the probability of the people in power being individuals who
> would dislike the possession and exercise of power is on a level with

the probability that an extremely tender-hearted person would get the job of whipping-master in a slave plantation.[1]

We cannot, however, exhaust this subject here.   The problem of the selection of the leaders is closely bound up with the wide problem of selection according to the opinions held, or rather according to the readiness with which a person conforms to an ever-changing set of doctrines.   And this leads us to one of the most characteristic moral features of totalitarianism, its relation to, and its effect on, all the virtues falling under the general heading of truthfulness.   This is so big a subject that it requires a separate chapter.

[1] Professor F. H. Knight in *The Journal of Political Economy*, December 1938, p. 869.

CHAPTER XI

THE END OF TRUTH

It is significant that the nationalisation of thought has proceeded everywhere *pari passu* with the nationalisation of industry.

E. H. Carr.

THE most effective way of making everybody serve the single system of ends towards which the social plan is directed is to make everybody believe in those ends. To make a totalitarian system function efficiently it is not enough that everybody should be forced to work for the same ends. It is essential that the people should come to regard them as their own ends. Although the beliefs must be chosen for the people and imposed upon them, they must become their beliefs, a generally accepted creed which makes the individuals as far as possible act spontaneously in the way the planner wants. If the feeling of oppression in totalitarian countries is in general much less acute than most people in liberal countries imagine, this is because the totalitarian governments succeed to a high degree in making people think as they want them to.

This is, of course, brought about by the various forms of propaganda. Its technique is now so familiar that we need say little about it. The only point that needs to be stressed is that neither propaganda in itself, nor the techniques employed, are peculiar to totalitarianism, and that what so completely changes its nature and effect in a totalitarian state is that all propaganda serves the same goal, that all the instruments of propaganda are co-ordinated to influence the individuals in the same direction and to produce the characteristic *Gleichschaltung* of all minds. As a result, the effect of propaganda in totalitarian countries is different not only in magnitude but in kind from that of the propaganda made for different ends by independent and competing agencies. If all the sources of current information are effectively under one single control, it is no longer a question of merely persuading the people of this or that. The skilful propagandist then has power to mould their minds in any direction he chooses and even the most intelligent and independent people cannot entirely escape that influence if they are long isolated from all other sources of information.

While in the totalitarian states this status of propaganda gives it a unique power over the minds of the people, the peculiar moral effects arise not from the technique but from the object and scope

of totalitarian propaganda. If it could be confined to indoctrinat-
ing the people with the whole system of values towards which
the social effort is directed, propaganda would represent merely
a particular manifestation of the characteristic features of collectivist morals which we have already considered. If its object
were merely to teach the people a definite and comprehensive
moral code, the problem would be solely whether this moral code
is good or bad. We have seen that the moral code of a totalitarian
society is not likely to appeal to us, that even the striving for
equality by means of a directed economy can only result in an
officially enforced inequality—an authoritarian determination of
the status of each individual in the new hierarchical order ; that
most of the humanitarian elements of our morals, the respect
for human life, for the weak and for the individual generally,
will disappear. However repellent this may be to most people,
and though it involves a change in moral standards, it is not
necessarily entirely anti-moral. Some features of such a system
may even appeal to the sternest moralists of a conservative
tint and seem to them preferable to the softer standards of a
liberal society.

The moral consequences of totalitarian propaganda which we
must now consider are, however, of an even more profound kind.
They are destructive of all morals because they undermine one
of the foundations of all morals, the sense of and the respect for
truth. From the nature of its task, totalitarian propaganda cannot
confine itself to values, to questions of opinion and moral convictions in which the individual always will conform more or less
to the views ruling his community, but must extend to questions
of fact where human intelligence is involved in a different way.
This is so, firstly, because in order to induce people to accept the
official values, these must be justified, or shown to be connected
with the values already held by the people, which usually will
involve assertions about causal connections between means and
ends ; and, secondly, because the distinction between ends and
means, between the goal aimed at and the measures taken to
achieve it, is in fact never so clear-cut and definite as any general
discussion of these problems is apt to suggest ; and because,
therefore, people must be brought to agree not only with the
ultimate aims but also with the views about the facts and possibilities on which the particular measures are based.

 *   *   *   *   *

We have seen that agreement on that complete ethical code,
that all-comprehensive system of values which is implicit in an
economic plan, does not exist in a free society but would have
to be created. But we must not assume that the planner will

approach his task aware of that need, or that, even if he were aware of it, it would be possible to create such a comprehensive code in advance. He only finds out about the conflicts between different needs as he goes along, and has to make his decisions as the necessity arises. The code of values guiding his decisions does not exist *in abstracto* before the decisions have to be made, it has to be created with the particular decisions. We have also seen how this inability to separate the general problem of values from the particular decisions makes it impossible that a democratic body, while unable to decide the technical details of a plan, should yet determine the values guiding it.

And while the planning authority will constantly have to decide issues on merits about which there exist no definite moral rules, it will have to justify its decisions to the people—or, at least, have somehow to make the people believe that they are the right decisions. Although those responsible for a decision may have been guided by no more than prejudice, some guiding principle will have to be stated publicly if the community is not merely passively to submit but actively to support the measure. The need to rationalise the likes and dislikes which, for lack of anything else, must guide the planner in many of his decisions, and the necessity of stating his reasons in a form in which they will appeal to as many people as possible, will force him to construct theories, i.e. assertions about the connections between facts, which then become an integral part of the governing doctrine. This process of creating a " myth " to justify his action need not be conscious. The totalitarian leader may be guided merely by an instinctive dislike of the state of things he has found and a desire to create a new hierarchical order which conforms better to his conception of merit, he may merely know that he dislikes the Jews who seemed to be so successful in an order which did not provide a satisfactory place for him, and that he loves and admires the tall blond man, the " aristocratic " figure of the novels of his youth. So he will readily embrace theories which seem to provide a rational justification for the prejudices which he shares with many of his fellows. Thus a pseudo-scientific theory becomes part of the official creed which to a greater or lesser degree directs everybody's action. Or the widespread dislike of the industrial civilisation and a romantic yearning for country life, together with a (probably erroneous) idea about the special value of country people as soldiers, provides the basis for another myth : *Blut und Boden* (blood and soil), expresses not merely ultimate values but a whole host of beliefs about cause and effect which once they have become ideals directing the activity of the whole community must not be questioned.

The need for such official doctrines as an instrument of directing and rallying the efforts of the people has been clearly foreseen by the various theoreticians of the totalitarian system. Plato's "noble lies" and Sorel's "myths" serve the same purpose as the racial doctrine of the Nazis or the theory of the corporative state of Mussolini. They are all necessarily based on particular views about facts which are then elaborated into scientific theories in order to justify a preconceived opinion.

* * * * *

The most effective way of making people accept the validity of the values they are to serve is to persuade them that they are really the same as those which they, or at least the best among them, have always held, but which were not properly understood or recognised before. The people are made to transfer their allegiance from the old gods to the new under the pretence that the new gods really are what their sound instinct had always told them but what before they had only dimly seen. And the most efficient technique to this end is to use the old words but change their meaning. Few traits of totalitarian regimes are at the same time so confusing to the superficial observer and yet so characteristic of the whole intellectual climate as the complete perversion of language, the change of meaning of the words by which the ideals of the new regimes are expressed.

The worst sufferer in this respect is, of course, the word liberty. It is a word used as freely in totalitarian states as elsewhere. Indeed it could almost be said—and it should serve as a warning to us to be on our guard against all the tempters who promise us *New Liberties for Old* [1]—that wherever liberty as we understand it has been destroyed, this has almost always been done in the name of some new freedom promised to the people. Even among us we have " planners for freedom " who promise us a " collective freedom for the group ", the nature of which may be gathered from the fact that its advocate finds it necessary to assure us that " naturally the advent of planned freedom does not mean that all [*sic*] earlier forms of freedom must be abolished ". Dr. Karl Mannheim, from whose work [2] these sentences are taken, at least warns us that " a conception of freedom modelled on the preceding age is an obstacle to any real understanding of the problem ". But his use of the word freedom is as misleading as it is in the mouth of totalitarian politicians. Like their freedom the " collective freedom " he offers us is not the freedom of the members of society but the unlimited freedom of the planner to

[1] This is the title of a recent work by the American historian C. L. Becker.
[2] *Man and Society in an Age of Reconstruction*, p. 377.

do with society what he pleases.[1] It is the confusion of freedom with power carried to the extreme.

In this particular case the perversion of the meaning of the word has, of course, been well prepared by a long line of German philosophers, and not least by many of the theoreticians of socialism. But freedom or liberty are by no means the only words whose meaning has been changed into their opposites to make them serve as instruments of totalitarian propaganda. We have already seen how the same happens to justice and law, right and equality. The list could be extended till it includes almost all moral and political terms in general use.

If one has not oneself experienced this process, it is difficult to appreciate the magnitude of this change of the meaning of words, the confusion which it causes, and the barriers to any rational discussion which it creates. It has to be seen to be understood how, if one of two brothers embraces the new faith, after a short while he appears to speak a different language which makes any real communication between them impossible. And the confusion becomes worse because this change of meaning of the words describing political ideals is not a single event but a continuous process, a technique employed consciously or unconsciously to direct the people. Gradually, as this process continues, the whole language becomes despoiled, words become empty shells deprived of any definite meaning, as capable of denoting one thing as its opposite and used solely for the emotional associations which still adhere to them.

*　　*　　*　　*　　*

It is not difficult to deprive the great majority of independent thought. But the minority who will retain an inclination to criticise must also be silenced. We have already seen why coercion cannot be confined to the acceptance of the ethical code underlying the plan according to which all social activity is directed. Since many parts of this code will never be explicitly stated, since many parts of the guiding scale of values will exist only implicitly in the plan, the plan itself in every detail, in fact every act of the government, must become sacrosanct and exempt from criticism. If the people are to support the common effort without hesitation, they must be convinced that not only the end aimed at but also the means chosen are the right ones. The official creed, to which adherence must be enforced, will therefore

---

[1] Mr. Peter Drucker (*The End of Economic Man*, p. 74) correctly observes that " the less freedom there is, the more there is talk of the ' new freedom '. Yet this new freedom is a mere word which covers the exact contradiction of all that Europe ever understood by freedom. . . . The new freedom which is preached in Europe is, however, the right of the majority against the individual."

comprise all the views about facts on which the plan is based. Public criticism or even expressions of doubt must be suppressed because they tend to weaken public support. As the Webbs report of the position in every Russian enterprise : " Whilst the work is in progress, any public expression of doubt, or even fear that the plan will not be successful, is an act of disloyalty and even of treachery because of its possible effects on the will and on the efforts of the rest of the staff." [1] When the doubt or fear expressed concerns not the success of a particular enterprise but of the whole social plan, it must even more be treated as sabotage.

Facts and theories must thus become no less the object of an official doctrine than views about values. And the whole apparatus for spreading knowledge, the schools and the press, wireless and cinema, will be used exclusively to spread those views which, whether true or false, will strengthen the belief in the rightness of the decisions taken by the authority ; and all information that might cause doubt or hesitation will be withheld. The probable effect on the people's loyalty to the system becomes the only criterion for deciding whether a particular piece of information is to be published or suppressed. The situation in a totalitarian state is permanently and in all fields the same that it is elsewhere in some fields in wartime. Everything which might cause doubt about the wisdom of the government or create discontent will be kept from the people. The basis of unfavourable comparisons with conditions elsewhere, the knowledge of possible alternatives to the course actually taken, information which might suggest failure on the part of the government to live up to its promises or to take advantage of opportunities to improve conditions, will all be suppressed. There is consequently no field where the systematic control of information will not be practised and uniformity of views not enforced.

This applies even to fields apparently most remote from any political interests, and particularly to all the sciences, even the most abstract. That in the disciplines dealing directly with human affairs and therefore most immediately affecting political views, such as history, law, or economics, the disinterested search for truth cannot be allowed in a totalitarian system, and the vindication of the official views becomes the sole object, is easily seen and has been amply confirmed by experience. These disciplines have indeed in all totalitarian countries become the most fertile factories of the official myths which the rulers use to guide the minds and wills of their subjects. It is not surprising that in these spheres even the pretence that they search for truth is abandoned and that the authorities decide what doctrines ought to be taught and published.

[1] S. and B. Webb, *Soviet Communism*, p. 1038.

Totalitarian control of opinion extends, however, also to subjects which at first seem to have no political significance. Sometimes it is difficult to explain why particular doctrines should be officially proscribed or why others should be encouraged, and it is curious that these likes and dislikes are apparently somewhat similar in the different totalitarian systems. In particular, they all seem to have in common an intense dislike of the more abstract forms of thought—a dislike characteristically also shown by many of the collectivists among our scientists. Whether the theory of relativity is represented as a " semitic attack on the foundation of Christian and Nordic physics " or opposed because it is " in conflict with dialectical materialism and Marxist dogma " comes very much to the same thing. Nor does it make much difference whether certain theorems of mathematical statistics are attacked because they " form part of the class struggle on the ideological frontier and are a product of the historical rôle of mathematics as the servant of the bourgeoisie ", or whether the whole subject is condemned because " it provides no guarantee that it will serve the interest of the people ". It seems that pure mathematics is no less a victim and that even the holding of particular views about the nature of continuity can be ascribed to " bourgeois prejudices ". According to the Webbs the *Journal for Marxist-Leninist Natural Sciences* has the following slogans : " We stand for Party in Mathematics. We stand for the purity of Marxist-Leninist theory in surgery." The situation seems to be very similar in Germany. The *Journal of the National-Socialist Association of Mathematicians* is full of " party in mathematics ", and one of the best known German physicists, the Nobel prizeman Lennard, has summed up his life work under the title *German Physics in Four Volumes* !

It is entirely in keeping with the whole spirit of totalitarianism that it condemns any human activity done for its own sake and without ulterior purpose. Science for science' sake, art for art's sake, are equally abhorrent to the Nazis, our socialist intellectuals, and the communists. *Every* activity must derive its justification from a conscious social purpose. There must be no spontaneous, unguided activity, because it might produce results which cannot be foreseen and for which the plan does not provide. It might produce something new, undreamt of in the philosophy of the planner. The principle extends even to games and amusements. I leave it to the reader to guess whether it was in Germany or in Russia where chess-players were officially exhorted that " we must finish once and for all with the neutrality of chess. We must condemn once and for all the formula ' chess for the sake of chess ' like the formula ' art for art's sake ' ".

Incredible as some of these aberrations may appear, we must

yet be on our guard not to dismiss them as mere accidental by-products which have nothing to do with the essential character of a planned or totalitarian system. They are not. They are a direct result of that same desire to see everything directed by a " unitary conception of the whole ", of the need to uphold at all costs the views in the service of which people are asked to make constant sacrifices, and of the general idea that the knowledge and beliefs of the people are an instrument to be used for a single purpose. Once science has to serve, not truth, but the interests of a class, a community, or a state, the sole task of argument and discussion is to vindicate and to spread still further the beliefs by which the whole life of the community is directed. As the Nazi Minister of Justice has explained, the question which every new scientific theory must ask itself is : " Do I serve National-Socialism for the greatest benefit of all ? "

The word truth itself ceases to have its old meaning. It describes no longer something to be found, with the individual conscience as the sole arbiter of whether in any particular instance the evidence (or the standing of those proclaiming it) warrants a belief ; it becomes something to be laid down by authority, something which has to be believed in the interest of the unity of the organised effort, and which may have to be altered as the exigencies of this organised effort require it.

The general intellectual climate which this produces, the spirit of complete cynicism as regards truth which it engenders, the loss of the sense of even the meaning of truth, the disappearance of the spirit of independent inquiry and of the belief in the power of rational conviction, the way in which differences of opinion in every branch of knowledge become political issues to be decided by authority, are all things which one must personally experience— no short description can convey their extent. Perhaps the most alarming fact is that contempt for intellectual liberty is not a thing which arises only once the totalitarian system is established, but one which can be found everywhere among intellectuals who have embraced a collectivist faith and who are acclaimed as intellectual leaders even in countries still under a liberal regime. Not only is even the worst oppression condoned if it is committed in the name of socialism, and the creation of a totalitarian system openly advocated by people who pretend to speak for the scientists of liberal countries ; intolerance too is openly extolled. Have we not recently seen a British scientific writer defend even Inquisition because in his opinion it " is beneficial to science when it protects a rising class " ? [1] This view is, of course, practically indistinguishable from the views which led the Nazis to the persecution of men of science, the burning of scientific books,

[1] J. G. Crowther, *The Social Relations of Science*, 1941, p. 333.

and the systematic eradication of the intelligentsia of the subjected
people.

*   *   *   *   *

The desire to force upon the people a creed which is regarded
as salutary for them is, of course, not a thing that is new or
peculiar to our time.   New, however, is the argument by which
many of our intellectuals try to justify such attempts.   There is
no real freedom of thought in our society, so it is said, because
the opinions and tastes of the masses are shaped by propaganda,
by advertising, by the example of the upper classes, and by other
environmental factors which inevitably force the thinking of the
people into well-worn grooves.   From this it is concluded that
if the ideals and tastes of the great majority are always fashioned
by circumstances which we can control, we ought to use this
power deliberately to turn the thoughts of the people in what
we think is a desirable direction.

Probably it is true enough that the great majority are rarely
capable of thinking independently, that on most questions they
accept views which they find ready-made, and that they will be
equally content if born or coaxed into one set of beliefs or another.
In any society freedom of thought will probably be of direct
significance only for a small minority.   But this does not mean
that anyone is competent, or ought to have power, to select those
to whom this freedom is to be reserved.   It certainly does not
justify the presumption of any group of people to claim the right
to determine what people ought to think or believe.   It shows a
complete confusion of thought to suggest that, because under any
sort of system the majority of people follow the lead of somebody,
it makes no difference if everybody has to follow the same lead.
To deprecate the value of intellectual freedom because it will
never mean for everybody the same possibility of independent
thought is completely to miss the reasons which give intellectual
freedom its value.   What is essential to make it serve its function
as the prime mover of intellectual progress is not that everybody
may be able to think or write anything, but that any cause or
idea may be argued by somebody.   So long as dissent is not
suppressed, there will always be some who will query the ideas
ruling their contemporaries and put new ideas to the test of
argument and propaganda.

This interaction of individuals, possessing different knowledge
and different views, is what constitutes the life of thought.   The
growth of reason is a social process based on the existence of
such differences.   It is of its essence that its results cannot be
predicted, that we cannot know which views will assist this growth
and which will not—in short, that this growth cannot be governed

by any views which we now possess without at the same time limiting it. To " plan " or " organise " the growth of mind, or, for that matter, progress in general, is a contradiction in terms. The idea that the human mind ought " consciously " to control its own development confuses individual reason, which alone can " consciously control " anything, with the interpersonal process to which its growth is due. By attempting to control it we are merely setting bounds to its development and must sooner or later produce a stagnation of thought and a decline of reason.

The tragedy of collectivist thought is that while it starts out to make reason supreme, it ends by destroying reason because it misconceives the process on which the growth of reason depends. It may indeed be said that it is the paradox of all collectivist doctrine and its demand for the " conscious " control or " conscious " planning that they necessarily lead to the demand that the mind of some individual should rule supreme—while only the individualist approach to social phenomena makes us recognise the super-individual forces which guide the growth of reason. Individualism is thus an attitude of humility before this social process and of tolerance to other opinions, and is the exact opposite of that intellectual hubris which is at the root of the demand for comprehensive direction of the social process.

CHAPTER XII

THE SOCIALIST ROOTS OF NAZISM

> All anti-liberal forces are combining against everything that
> is liberal.
>
> *A. Moeller van den Bruck.*

IT is a common mistake to regard National-Socialism as a mere
revolt against reason, an irrational movement without intellectual
background. If that were so, the movement would be much less
dangerous than it is. But nothing could be further from the
truth or more misleading. The doctrines of National-Socialism
are the culmination of a long evolution of thought, a process
in which thinkers who have had great influence far beyond
the confines of Germany have taken part. Whatever one may
think of the premises from which they started, it cannot be denied
that the men who produced the new doctrines were powerful
writers who left the impress of their ideas on the whole of
European thought. Their system was developed with ruthless
consistency. Once one accepts the premises from which it
starts, there is no escape from its logic. It is simply collectivism
freed from all traces of an individualist tradition which might
hamper its realisation.

Though in this development German thinkers have taken the
lead, they were by no means alone. Thomas Carlyle and Houston
Stewart Chamberlain, Auguste Comte and Georges Sorel are as
much a part of that continuous development as any Germans.
The development of this strand of thought within Germany has
been well traced recently by Mr. R. D. Butler in his study of
The Roots of National Socialism. But although its persistence
there through a hundred and fifty years in almost unchanged
and ever-recurring form, which emerges from that study, is rather
frightening, it is easy to exaggerate the importance these ideas
had in Germany before 1914. They were only one strand of
thought among a people then perhaps more varied in its views
than any other. And they were on the whole represented by a
small minority and held in as great contempt by the majority of
Germans as they were in other countries.

What, then, caused these views held by a reactionary minority
finally to gain the support of the great majority of Germans
and practically the whole of her youth ? It was not merely
the defeat, the suffering, and the wave of nationalism which
led to their success. Still less was the cause, as so many people
wish to believe, a capitalist reaction against the advance of

socialism. On the contrary, the support which brought these ideas to power came precisely from the socialist camp. It was certainly not through the bourgeoisie, but rather the absence of a strong bourgeoisie, by which they were helped to power.

The doctrines which had guided the ruling elements in Germany for the past generation were not opposed to the socialism in Marxism, but to the liberal elements contained in it, its internationalism and its democracy. And as it became increasingly clear that it was just these elements which formed obstacles to the realisation of socialism, the socialists of the left approached more and more to those of the right. It was the union of the anti-capitalist forces of the right and the left, the fusion of radical and conservative socialism, which drove out from Germany everything that was liberal.

The connection between socialism and nationalism in Germany was close from the beginning. It is significant that the most important ancestors of National-Socialism—Fichte, Rodbertus, and Lassalle—are at the same time acknowledged fathers of socialism. While theoretical socialism in its Marxist form was directing the German labour movement, the authoritarian and nationalist element receded for a time into the background. But not for long.[1] From 1914 onwards there arose from the ranks of Marxist socialism one teacher after another who led, not the conservatives and reactionaries, but the hardworking labourer and idealist youth into the national-socialist fold. It was only thereafter that the tide of nationalist socialism attained major importance and rapidly grew into the Hitlerian doctrine. The war hysteria of 1914, which, just because of the German defeat, was never fully cured, is the beginning of the modern development which produced National-Socialism, and it was largely with the assistance of old socialists that it rose during this period.

* * * * *

Perhaps the first, and in some ways the most characteristic, representative of this development is the late Professor Werner Sombart, whose notorious *Händler und Helden* (Merchants and Heroes) appeared in 1915. Sombart had begun as a Marxian socialist, and as late as 1909 could assert with pride that he had devoted the greater part of his life to fighting for the ideas of Karl Marx. He had done as much as any man to spread socialist ideas and anti-capitalist resentment of varying shades throughout

[1] And only partially. In 1892 one of the leaders of the social-democratic party, August Bebel, was able to tell Bismarck that " the Imperial Chancellor can rest assured that German Social Democracy is a sort of preparatory school for militarism " !

Germany; and if German thought became penetrated with
Marxian elements in a way that was true of no other country till
the Russian revolution, this was in a large measure due to Sombart.
At one time he was regarded as the outstanding representative of
the persecuted socialist intelligentsia, unable, because of his
radical views, to obtain a University chair. And even after the
last war the influence, inside and outside Germany of his work
as a historian, which remained Marxist in approach after he had
ceased to be a Marxist in politics, was most extensive and is
particularly noticeable in the works of many of the English and
American planners.

In his war book this old socialist welcomed the " German
War " as the inevitable conflict between the commercial civilisation
of England and the heroic culture of Germany. His contempt
for the " commercial " views of the English people, who had
lost all warlike instincts, is unlimited. Nothing is more contemptible in his eyes than the universal striving after the happiness
of the individual; and what he describes as the leading maxim
of English morals : be just " that it may be well with thee and
that thou mayest prolong thy days upon the land " is to him " the
most infamous maxim which has ever been pronounced by a commercial mind ". The " German idea of the state " as formulated
by Fichte, Lassalle, and Rodbertus, is that the state is neither
founded nor formed by individuals, nor an aggregate of individuals,
nor is its purpose to serve any interest of individuals. It is
a *Volksgemeinschaft* in which the individual has no rights but
only duties. Claims of the individual are always an outcome
of the commercial spirit. " The ideas of 1789 "—Liberty,
Equality Fraternity—are characteristically commercial ideals
which have no other purpose but to secure certain advantages
to individuals.

Before 1914 all the true German ideals of a heroic life were
in deadly danger before the continuous advance of English commercial ideals, English comfort, and English sport. The English
people had not only themselves become completely corrupted,
every trade unionist being sunk in the " morass of comfort ",
but they had begun to infect all other peoples. Only the war had
helped the Germans to remember that they were really a people
of warriors, a people among whom all activities and particularly all
economic activities were subordinated to military ends. Sombart
knew that the Germans were held in contempt by other people
because they regard war as sacred—but he glories in it. To regard
war as inhuman and senseless is a product of commercial views.
There is a life higher than the individual life, the life of the people
and the life of the state, and it is the purpose of the individual
to sacrifice himself for that higher life. War is to Sombart the

consummation of the heroic view of life, and the war against England is the war against the opposite ideal, the commercial ideal of individual freedom and of English comfort, which in his eyes finds its most contemptible expression in—the safety-razors found in the English trenches.

*   *   *   *   *

If Sombart's outburst was at the time too much even for most Germans, another German professor arrived at essentially the same ideas in a more moderate and more scholarly, but for that reason even more effective, form. Professor Johann Plenge was as great an authority on Marx as Sombart. His book on *Marx und Hegel* marks the beginning of the modern Hegel-renaissance among Marxian scholars ; and there can be no doubt about the genuinely socialist nature of the convictions with which he started. Among his numerous war publications the most important is a small but at the time widely discussed book with the significant title : *1789 and 1914. The Symbolic Years in the History of the Political Mind.* It is devoted to the conflict between the " Ideas of 1789 ", the ideal of freedom, and the " Ideas of 1914 ", the ideal of organisation. Organisation is to him, as to all socialists who derive their socialism from a crude application of scientific ideals to the problems of society, the essence of socialism. It was, as he rightly emphasises, the root of the socialist movement at its inception in early nineteenth-century France. Marx and Marxism have betrayed this basic idea of socialism by their fanatic but utopian adherence to the abstract idea of freedom. Only now was the idea of organisation again coming into its own, elsewhere, as witnessed by the work of Mr. H. G. Wells (by whose *Future in America* Professor Plenge was profoundly influenced, and whom he describes as one of the outstanding figures of modern socialism), but particularly in Germany, where it is best understood and most fully realised. The war between England and Germany is therefore really a conflict between two opposite principles. The " Economic World War " is the third great epoch of spiritual struggle in modern history. It is of equal importance with the Reformation and the bourgeois revolution of liberty. It is the struggle for the victory of the new forces born out of the advanced economic life of the nineteenth century : socialism and organisation.

Because in the sphere of ideas Germany was the most convinced exponent of all socialist dreams, and in the sphere of reality she was the most powerful architect of the most highly organised economic system.—In us is the twentieth century. However the war may end, we are the exemplary people. Our ideas will determine the aims of the life of humanity.—World History experiences at present the colossal spectacle that with us a new great ideal of life penetrates to final victory, while at the same time in England one of the World-Historical principles finally collapses.

The war economy created in Germany in 1914

is the first realisation of a socialist society and its spirit the first active, and not merely demanding, appearance of a socialist spirit. The needs of the war have established the socialist idea in German economic life, and thus the defence of our nation produced for humanity the idea of 1914, the idea of German organisation, the people's community (*Volksgemeinschaft*) of national socialism. . . . Without our really noticing it the whole of our political life in state and industry has risen to a higher stage.   State and economic life form a new unity. . . .   The feeling of economic responsibility which characterises the work of the civil servant pervades all private activity. . . .   The new German corporative constitution of economic life [which Professor Plenge admits is not yet ripe or. complete] is the highest form of life of the state which has ever been known on earth.

At first Professor Plenge still hoped to reconcile the ideal of liberty and the ideal of organisation, although largely through the complete but voluntary submission of the individual to the whole. But these traces of liberal ideas soon disappear from his writings. By 1918 the union between socialism and ruthless power politics had become complete in his mind.   Shortly before the end of the war he exhorted his compatriots in the socialist journal *Die Glocke* in the following manner :

It is high time to recognise the fact that socialism must be power policy, because it is to be organisation.   Socialism has to win power : it must never blindly destroy power.   And the most important and critical question for socialism in the time of war of peoples is necessarily this : what people is pre-eminently summoned to power, because it is the exemplary leader in the organisation of peoples ?

And he forecast all the ideas which were finally to justify Hitler's New Order :

Just from the point of view of socialism, which is organisation, is not an absolute right of self-determination of the peoples the right of individualistic economic anarchy ?   Are we willing to grant complete self-determination to the individual in economic life ?   Consistent socialism can accord to the people a right to incorporation only in accordance with the real distribution of forces historically determined.

*   *   *   *   *

The ideals which Plenge expressed so clearly were especially popular among, and perhaps even derive from, certain circles

of German scientists and engineers who, precisely as is now
so loudly demanded by their English counterparts, clamoured for
the centrally planned organisation of all aspects of life.   Leading
among these was the famous chemist Wilhelm Ostwald, one
of whose pronouncements on this point has achieved a certain
celebrity.   He is reported to have stated publicly that

> Germany wants to organise Europe which up to now still
> lacks organisation.   I will explain to you now Germany's great
> secret : we, or perhaps the German race, have discovered the
> significance of organisation.   While the other nations still live
> under the regime of individualism, we have already achieved that
> of organisation.

Ideas very similar to these were current in the offices of the
German raw material dictator, Walter Rathenau, who, although
he would have shuddered had he realised the consequences of
his totalitarian economics, yet deserves a considerable place in
any fuller history of the growth of Nazi ideas.   Through his
writings he has probably, more than any other man, determined
the economic views of the generation which grew up in Germany
during and immediately after the last war ; and some of his
closest collaborators were later to form the backbone of the staff
of Goering's Five Year Plan administration.   Very similar also
was much of the teaching of another former Marxist, Friedrich
Naumann, whose *Mitteleuropa* reached probably the greatest
circulation of any war book in Germany.[1]   But it was left to an
active socialist politician, a member of the left wing of the social-
democratic party in the Reichstag, to develop these ideas most
fully and to spread them far and wide.   Paul Lensch had already
in earlier books described the war as " the flight of the English
bourgeoisie before the advance of socialism ", and explained how
different were the socialist ideal of freedom and the Englis
conception.   But only in his third and most successful war book,
his *Three Years of World Revolution*,[2] were his characteristic
ideas, under the influence of Plenge, to achieve full development.   Lensch bases his argument on an interesting and in
many respects accurate historical account of how the adoption
of protection by Bismarck had made possible in Germany a
development towards that industrial concentration and cartellisa-
tion which, from his Marxist standpoint, represented a higher
state of industrial development.

[1] A good summary of Naumann's views, as characteristic of the German
combination of Socialism and Imperialism as any we quote in the text,
will be found in R. D. Butler, *The Roots of National Socialism*, 1941, pp.
203–9.
[2] Paul Lensch, *Three Years of World Revolution*.   Preface by J. E. M., London, 1918.   The English translation of this work was made available, still
during the last war, by some far-seeing person.

The result of Bismarck's decision of the year 1879 was that Germany took on the rôle of the revolutionary; that is to say, of a state whose position in relation to the rest of the world is that of a representative of a higher and more advanced economic system. Having realised this, we should perceive that *in the present World Revolution Germany represents the revolutionary, and her greatest antagonist, England, the counter-revolutionary side.* This fact proves how little the constitution of a country, whether it be liberal and republican or monarchic and autocratic, affects the question whether, from the point of view of historical development, that country is to be regarded as liberal or not. Or, to put it more plainly, our conceptions of Liberalism, Democracy, and so forth, are derived from the ideas of English Individualism, according to which a state with a weak government is a liberal state, and every restriction upon the freedom of the individual is conceived as the product of autocracy and militarism.

In Germany, the " historically appointed representative " of this higher form of economic life,

the struggle for socialism has been extraordinarily simplified, since all the prerequisite conditions of Socialism had already become established there. And hence it was necessarily a vital concern of any socialist party that Germany should triumphantly hold her own against her enemies, and thereby be able to fulfil her historic mission of revolutionising the world. Hence the war of the Entente against Germany resembled the attempt of the lower bourgeoisie of the pre-capitalistic age to prevent the decline of their own class.

That organisation of Capital [Lensch continues] which began unconsciously before the war, and which during the war has been continued consciously, will be systematically continued after the war. Not through any desire for any arts of organisation nor yet because socialism has been recognised as a higher principle of social development. The classes who are to-day the practical pioneers of socialism are, in theory, its avowed opponents, or, at any rate, were so up to a short time ago. Socialism is coming, and in fact has to some extent already arrived, since we can no longer live without it.

The only people who still oppose this tendency are the liberals.

This class of people, who unconsciously reason from English standards, comprises the whole educated German bourgeoisie. Their political notions of " freedom " and " civic right ", of constitutionalism and parliamentarianism, are derived from that individualistic conception of the world, of which English Liberalism is a classical embodiment, and which was adopted by the spokesmen of the German bourgeoisie in the 'fifties, 'sixties, and 'seventies of the nineteenth century. But these standards are old-fashioned and shattered, just as old-fashioned English Liberalism has been shattered by this war. What has to be done now is to get rid of these inherited political ideas and to assist the growth of a new conception of State

and Society.   In this sphere also Socialism must present a conscious
and determined opposition to individualism.   In this connection it
is an astonishing fact that, in the so-called " reactionary " Germany,
the working classes have won for themselves a much more solid and
powerful position in the life of the state than is the case either in
England or in France.

Lensch follows this up with a consideration which again
contains much truth and which deserves to be pondered :

> Since the Social Democrats, by the aid of this [universal] suffrage,
> occupied every post which they could obtain in the Reichstag, the
> State Parliament, the municipal councils, the courts for the settlement
> of trade disputes, the sick funds, and so forth, they penetrated very
> deeply into the organism of the state ; but the price which they had
> to pay for this was that the state, in its turn, exercised a profound
> influence upon the working classes.   To be sure, as the result of
> strenuous socialistic labours for fifty years, the state is no longer the
> same as it was in the year 1867, when universal suffrage first came
> into operation ; but then, Social Democracy, in its turn, is no longer
> the same as it was at the time.   *The state has undergone a process
> of socialisation, and Social Democracy has undergone a process of
> nationalisation.*

*   *   *   *   *

Plenge and Lensch in turn have provided the leading ideas for
the immediate masters of National-Socialism, particularly Oswald
Spengler and A. Moeller van den Bruck, to mention only the two
best-known names.[1]   Opinions may differ in how far the former
can be regarded as a socialist.   But that in his tract on *Prussianism
and Socialism*, which appeared in 1920, he merely gave expression
to ideas widely held by German socialists will now be evident.
A few specimens of his argument will suffice.   " Old Prussian
spirit and socialist conviction, which to-day hate each other with
the hatred of brothers, are one and the same."   The representatives of Western civilisation in Germany, the German
liberals, are " the invisible English army which after the battle
of Jena, Napoleon left behind on German soil ".   To Spengler,
men like Hardenberg and Humboldt and all the other liberal
reformers were " English ".   But this " English " spirit will
be turned out by the German revolution which began in
1914.

---

[1] The same applies to many others of the intellectual leaders of the generation
which has produced Nazism, such as Othmar Spann, Hans Freyer, Carl
Schmitt, and Ernst Jünger.   On these compare the interesting study by
Aurel Kolnai, *The War against the West*, 1938, which suffers, however, from
the defect that, by confining itself to the post-war period when these ideals had
already been taken over by the nationalists, it overlooks their socialist creators.

The three last nations of the Occident have aimed at three forms of existence, represented by famous watchwords: Freedom, Equality, Community. They appear in the political forms of liberal Parliamentarianism, social Democracy, and authoritarian socialism.[1] . . . The German, more correctly, Prussian, instinct is: the power belongs to the whole. . . . Everyone is given his place. One commands or obeys. This is, since the eighteenth century, authoritarian socialism, essentially illiberal and anti-democratic, in so far as English Liberalism and French Democracy are meant. . . . There are in Germany many hated and ill-reputed contrasts, but liberalism alone is contemptible on German soil.

The structure of the English nation is based on the distinction between rich and poor, that of the Prussian on that between command and obedience. The meaning of class distinction is accordingly fundamentally different in the two countries.

After pointing out the essential difference between the English competitive system and the Prussian system of " economic administration ", and after showing (consciously following Lensch) how since Bismarck the deliberate organisation of economic activity had progressively assumed more socialist forms, Spengler continues :

> In Prussia there existed a real state in the most ambitious meaning of the word. There could be, strictly speaking, no private persons. Everybody who lived within the system that worked with the precision of a clockwork, was in some way a link in it. The conduct of public business could therefore not be in the hands of private people, as is supposed by Parliamentarianism. It was an *Amt* and the responsible politician was a civil servant, a servant of the whole.

The " Prussian idea " requires that everybody should become a state official, that all wages and salaries be fixed by the state. The administration of all property, in particular, becomes a salaried function. The state of the future will be a *Beamtenstaat*. But

> the decisive question not only for Germany, but for the world, which must be solved *by* Germany *for* the world is : Is in future trade to govern the state, or the state to govern trade ? In the face of this question Prussianism and Socialism are the same . . . Prussianism and Socialism combat the England in our midst.

---

[1] This Spenglerian formula finds its echo in an often quoted statement of Carl Schmitt, the leading Nazi expert on constitutional law, according to which the evolution of government proceeds " in three dialectic stages : from the *absolute* state of the seventeenth and eighteenth centuries through the *neutral* state of the liberal nineteenth century to the *totalitarian* state in which state and society are identical " (C. Schmitt, *Der Hüter der Verfassung*, Tübingen, 1931, p. 79).

It was only a step from this for the patron-saint of National-Socialism Moeller van den Bruck to proclaim the World War a war between liberalism and socialism : " We have lost the war against the West. Socialism has lost it against Liberalism." [1] As with Spengler, liberalism is, therefore, the arch-enemy. Moeller van den Bruck glories in the fact that

> there are no liberals in Germany to-day ; there are young revolu-
> tionaries : there are young conservatives. But who would be a
> liberal ? . . . Liberalism is a philosophy of life from which German
> youth now turns with nausea, with wrath, with quite peculiar scorn,
> for there is none more foreign, more repugnant, more opposed to its
> philosophy. German youth to-day recognises the liberal *as the
> arch-enemy*.

Moeller van den Bruck's Third Reich was intended to give the Germans a socialism adapted to their nature and undefiled by Western liberal ideas. And so it did.

These writers were by no means isolated phenomena. As early as 1922 a detached observer could speak of a " peculiar and, on a first glance, surprising phenomenon " then to be observed in Germany :

> The fight against the capitalistic order, according to this view, is
> a continuation of the war against the Entente with the weapons of
> the spirit and of economic organisation, the way which leads to
> practical socialism, a return of the German people to their best and
> noblest traditions.[2]

Fight against liberalism in all its forms, liberalism that had defeated Germany, was the common idea which united socialists and conservatives in one common front. At first it was mainly in the German Youth Movement, almost entirely socialist in inspiration and outlook, where these ideas were most readily accepted and the fusion of socialism and nationalism completed. In the later 'twenties and till the advent to power of Hitler a circle of young men gathered round the journal *Die Tat* and led by Ferdinand Fried became the chief exponent of this tradition in the intellectual sphere. Fried's *Ende des Kapitalismus* is perhaps the most characteristic product of this group of *Edelnazis*, as they were known in Germany, and is particularly

---

[1] Moeller van den Bruck, *Sozialismus und Aussenpolitik*, 1933, pp. 87, 90, and 100. The articles here reprinted, particularly the article on " Lenin and Keynes " which discusses most fully the contention discussed in the text, were first published between 1919 and 1923.

[2] K. Pribram, " Deutscher Nationalismus und Deutscher Sozialismus ", in *Archiv für Sozialwissenschaft und Sozialpolitik*, vol. 49, 1922, pp. 298-9. The writer mentions as further examples the philosopher Max Scheler preaching " the socialist world mission of Germany ", and the Marxist K. Korsch writing on the spirit of the new *Volksgemeinschaft*, as arguing in the same vein.

disquieting because of its resemblance to so much of the literature which we see in England to-day, where we can watch the same drawing together of the socialists of the Left and the Right, and nearly the same contempt of all that is liberal in the old sense. " Conservative Socialism " (and, in other circles, " Religious Socialism ") was the slogan under which a large number of writers prepared the atmosphere in which " National-Socialism " succeeded. It is " conservative socialism " which is the dominant trend in this country now. Had the war against the Western powers " with the weapons of the spirit and of economic organisation " not almost succeeded before the real war began ?

CHAPTER XIII

THE TOTALITARIANS IN OUR MIDST

When authority presents itself in the guise of organisation it develops charms fascinating enough to convert communities of free people into totalitarian States.

The Times.

PROBABLY it is true that the very magnitude of the outrages committed by the totalitarian governments, instead of increasing the fear that such a system might one day arise in this country, has rather strengthened the assurance that it cannot happen here. When we look to Nazi Germany the gulf which separates us seems so immense that nothing that happens there can possess relevance for any possible development in this country. And the fact that the difference has steadily become greater seems to refute any suggestion that we may be moving in a similar direction. But let us not forget that fifteen years ago the possibility of such a thing happening in Germany would have appeared just as fantastic, not only to nine-tenths of the Germans themselves, but also to the most hostile foreign observers (however wise they may now pretend to have been).

As suggested earlier in these pages, however, it is not the present Germany but the Germany of twenty or thirty years ago to which conditions in this country show an ever-increasing resemblance. There are many features which were then regarded as " typically German " and which are now equally familiar in this country, and many symptoms that point to a further development in the same direction. We have already mentioned the most significant, the increasing similarity between the economic views of the Right and Left and their common opposition to the Liberalism that used to be the common basis of most English politics. We have the authority of Mr. Harold Nicolson for the statement that during the last Conservative government, among the back-benchers of the Conservative party " the most gifted . . . were all socialists at heart " ; [1] and there can be little question that, as in the days of the Fabians, many socialists have more sympathy with the Conservatives than with the Liberals. There are many other features closely related to this. The increasing veneration for the state, the admiration of power, and of bigness for bigness' sake, the enthusiasm for " organisation " of everything (we now call it planning), and that " inability to leave anything to the simple power of organic growth ", which even H. v. Treitschke

[1] *The Spectator*, April 12, 1940, p. 523.

135

deplored of in the Germans sixty years ago, are all scarcely less marked in this country now than they were in Germany.

How far in the last twenty years England has travelled on the German path is brought home to one with extraordinary vividness if one now reads some of the more serious discussions of the differences between British and German views on political and moral issues which appeared in this country during the last war. It is probably true to say that then the British public had in general a truer appreciation of these differences than it has now ; but while the people of this country were then proud of their distinctive tradition, there are few of the political views then regarded as characteristically English of which the majority of people in this country do not now seem half ashamed, if they do not positively repudiate them.   It is scarcely an exaggeration to say that the more typically English a writer on political or social problems then appeared to the world, the more is he to-day forgotten in his own country.   Men like Lord Morley or Henry Sidgwick, Lord Acton or A. V. Dicey, who were then admired in the world at large as outstanding examples of the political wisdom of liberal England, are to the present generation largely obsolete Victorians. Perhaps nothing shows this change more clearly than that, while there is no lack of sympathetic treatment of Bismarck in contemporary English literature, the name of Gladstone is rarely mentioned by the younger generation without a sneer over his Victorian morality and naïve utopianism.

I wish I could in a few paragraphs adequately convey the alarming impression gained from the perusal of a few of the English works on the ideas dominating the Germany of the last war, where almost every word could be applied to the views most conspicuous in current English literature.   I shall merely quote one brief passage by Lord Keynes, describing in 1915 the "nightmare" which he found expounded in a typical German work of that period : he describes how according to a German author

> even in peace industrial life must remain mobilised.   This is what he means by speaking of the "militarisation of our industrial life" [the title of the work reviewed].   Individualism must come to an end absolutely.   A system of regulations must be set up, the object of which is not the greater happiness of the individual (Professor Jaffé is not ashamed to say this in so many words), but the strengthening of the organised unity of the state for the object of attaining the maximum degree of efficiency (*Leistungsfähigkeit*), the influence of which on individual advantage is only indirect.—This hideous doctrine is enshrined in a sort of idealism.   The nation will grow into a "closed unity" and will become, in fact, what Plato declared it should be—"Der Mensch im Grossen".   In particular, the coming peace will bring with it a strengthening of the idea of State action in industry.

. . . Foreign investment, emigration, the industrial policy which
in recent years had regarded the whole world as a market, are
too dangerous. The old order of industry, which is dying to-day,
is based on Profit ; and the new Germany of the twentieth-century
Power without consideration of Profit is to make an end of that
system of Capitalism, which came over from England one hundred
years ago.[1]

Except that no English author has yet to my knowledge dared
openly to disparage individual happiness, is there a passage in
this which is not mirrored in much of contemporary English
literature ?

And, undoubtedly, not merely the ideas which in Germany and
elsewhere prepared totalitarianism, but also many of the principles
of totalitarianism itself are what exercises an increasing fascination
in many other countries. Although few people, if anybody, in
this country would probably be ready to swallow totalitarianism
whole, there are few single features which we have not yet been
advised by somebody or other to imitate. Indeed, there is
scarcely a leaf out of Hitler's book which somebody or other in
this country has not recommended us to take and use for our own
purposes. This applies particularly to many people who are
undoubtedly Hitler's mortal enemies because of one special feature
in his system. We should never forget that the anti-semitism of
Hitler has driven from his country, or turned into his enemies,
many people who in every respect are confirmed totalitarians of
the German type.[2]

No description in general terms can give an adequate idea of
the similarity of much of current English political literature to
the works which destroyed the belief in Western civilisation in
Germany and created the state of mind in which Nazism could
become successful. The similarity is even more one of the
temper with which the problems are approached than of the
specific arguments used—a similar readiness to break all cultural
ties with the past and to stake everything on the success of a
particular experiment. As was also true in Germany, most of

[1] *Economic Journal*, 1915, p. 450.
[2] Especially when we consider the proportion of former socialists who have
become Nazis it is important to remember that the true significance of this ratio
is seen only if we compare it, not with the total number of former socialists,
but with the number of those whose conversion would not in any case have
been prevented by their ancestry. In fact, one of the surprising features of
the political emigration from Germany is the comparatively small number of
refugees from the Left who are not " Jews " in the German sense of the term.—
How often do we not hear eulogies of the German system prefaced by some
statement such as the following with which at a recent conference an enumeration of the " features of the totalitarian technique of economic mobilisation
which are worth thinking about " was introduced : " Herr Hitler is not my
ideal—far from it. There are very pressing personal reasons why Herr Hitler
should not be my ideal, but . . ."

the works which are preparing the way for a totalitarian course in this country are the product of sincere idealists and often of men of considerable intellectual distinction. So, although it is invidious to single out particular persons as illustrations where similar views are advocated by hundreds of others, I see no other way of demonstrating effectively how far this development has actually advanced in this country. I shall deliberately choose as illustrations authors whose sincerity and disinterestedness are above suspicion. But though I hope in this way to show how the views from which totalitarianism springs are now rapidly spreading here, I stand little chance of conveying successfully the equally important similarity in the emotional atmosphere. An extensive investigation into all the subtle changes in thought and language would be necessary to make explicit what one readily enough recognises as symptoms of a familiar development. Through meeting the kind of people who talk about the necessity of opposing " big " ideas to " small " ones and of re-placing the old " static " or " partial " thinking by the new " dynamic " or " global " way one learns to recognise that what at first appears sheer nonsense is a sign of the same intellectual attitude with whose manifestations we can alone concern our-selves here.

*   *   *   *   *

My first examples are two works by a gifted scholar, which in the last few years have attracted much attention. There are, perhaps, few other instances in contemporary English literature where the influence of the specific German ideas with which we are concerned is so marked as in Professor E. H. Carr's books on the *Twenty Years' Crisis* and the *Conditions of Peace*.

In the first of these two books Professor Carr frankly confessed himself an adherent of " the ' historical school ' of realists [which] had its home in Germany and [whose] development can be traced through the great names of Hegel and Marx ". A realist, he explains, is one " who makes morality a function of politics " and who " cannot logically accept any standard of value save that of fact ". This " realism " is contrasted, in truly German fashion, with the " utopian " thought dating from the eighteenth century " which was essentially individualist in that it made the human conscience the final court of appeal ". But the old morals with their " abstract general principles " must disappear because " the empiricist treats the concrete case on its individual merits ". In other words, nothing but expediency matters, and we are even assured that " the rule *pacta sunt servanda* is not a moral principle ". That without abstract general principles merit becomes solely a matter of arbitrary opinion, and that international treaties, if they are not morally binding, have no meaning whatever, does not seem to worry Professor Carr.

According to Professor Carr, indeed, although he does not explicitly say so, it appears that England fought the last war on the wrong side.   Anyone who re-reads now the statements of British war aims of twenty-five years ago and compares them with Professor Carr's present views will readily see that what were then believed to be the German views are now those of Professor Carr who would presumably argue that the different views then professed in this country were merely a product of British hypocrisy.   How little difference he is able to see between the ideals held in this country and those practised by present-day Germany is best illustrated by his assertion that

> it is true that when a prominent National-Socialist asserts that " anything that benefits the German people is right, anything that harms them is wrong " he is merely propounding the same identifica- tion of national interest with universal right which has already been established for English-speaking countries by [President] Wilson, Professor Toynbee, Lord Cecil, and many others.

Since Professor Carr's books are devoted to international problems it is mainly in that field that their characteristic tendency becomes apparent.   But from the glimpses one gets of the char- acter of the future society which he contemplates, it appears also to be quite on the totalitarian model.   Sometimes one even wonders whether the resemblance is accidental or deliberate. Does Professor Carr, for example, realise, when he asserts that " we can no longer find much meaning in the distinction familiar to nineteenth-century thought between ' society ' and ' state ' ", that this is precisely the doctrine of Professor Carl Schmitt, the leading Nazi theoretician of totalitarianism, and, in fact, the essence of the definition of totalitarianism which that author has given to that term which he himself had introduced ?   Or that the view that " the mass production of opinion is the corollary of the mass-production of goods " and that, therefore, " the prejudice which the word propaganda still exerts in many minds to-day is closely parallel to the prejudice against control of industry and trade " is really an apology for a regimentation of opinion of the kind practised by the Nazis ?

In his more recent *Conditions of Peace* Professor Carr answers with an emphatic affirmative the question with which we con- cluded the last chapter :

> The victors lost the peace, and Soviet Russia and Germany won it, because the former continued to preach, and in part to apply, the once valid, but now disruptive ideals of the rights of nations and *laissez-faire* capitalism, whereas the latter, consciously or uncon-

sciously borne forward on the tide of the twentieth century, were striving to build up the world in larger units under centralised planning and control.

Professor Carr completely makes his own the German battle-cry of the socialist revolution of the East against the liberal West in which Germany was the leader :

> the revolution which began in the last war, which has been the driving force of every significant political movement in the last twenty years . . . a revolution against the predominant ideas of the nineteenth century : liberal democracy, national self-determination and *laissez-faire* economics.

As he himself rightly says " it was almost inevitable that this challenge to nineteenth-century beliefs which she had never really shared should find in Germany one of its strongest protagonists ". With all the fatalistic belief of every pseudo-historian since Hegel and Marx this development is represented as inevitable : " we know the direction in which the world is moving, and we must bow to it or perish."

The conviction that this trend is inevitable is characteristically based on familiar economic fallacies—the presumed necessity of the general growth of monopolies in consequence of technological developments, the alleged " potential plenty ", and all the other popular catchwords which appear in works of this kind. Professor Carr is not an economist and his economic argument generally will not bear serious examination. But neither this, nor his belief characteristically held at the same time, that the importance of the economic factor in social life is rapidly decreasing, prevent him from basing on economic arguments all his predictions about the inevitable developments or from presenting as his main demands for the future " the reinterpretation in predominantly economic terms of the democratic ideals of ' equality ' and ' liberty ' " !

Professor Carr's contempt for all the ideas of liberal economists (which he insists on calling nineteenth-century ideas, though he knows that Germany " had never really shared " them and had already in the nineteenth century practised most of the principles he now advocates), is as profound as that of any of the German writers quoted in the last chapter. He even takes over the German thesis, originated by Friedrich List, that Free Trade was a policy dictated solely by, and appropriate only to, the special interests of England in the nineteenth century. Now, however, " the artificial production of some degree of autarky is a necessary condition of orderly social existence ".. To bring about a " return to a more dispersed and generalised world trade . . . by a ' removal of trade barriers ' or by a resuscitation of the *laissez-*

faire principles of the nineteenth century " is " unthinkable ".
The future belongs to *Grossraumwirtschaft* of the German kind :
" the result which we desire can be won only by a deliberate
reorganisation of European life such as Hitler has undertaken " !

After all this one is hardly surprised to find a characteristic
section headed " The Moral Functions of War ", in which Professor Carr condescendingly pities " the well-meaning people
(especially in English-speaking countries) who, steeped in the
nineteenth-century tradition, persist in regarding war as senseless
and devoid of purpose ", and rejoices in the " sense of meaning
and purpose " which war, " the most powerful instrument of
social solidarity ", creates.   This is all very familiar—but it was
not in the works of English scholars that one expected to find
these views.

*   *   *   *   *

Possibly we have not yet given enough attention to one
feature of the intellectual development in Germany during the
last hundred years which is now in an almost identical form
making its appearance in this country : the scientists agitating
for a " scientific " organisation of society.   The ideal of a society
organised " through and through " from the top has in Germany
been considerably furthered by the quite unique influence which
her scientific and technological specialists were allowed to exercise
on the formation of social and political opinions.   Few people
remember that in the modern history of Germany the political
professors have played a rôle comparable to that of the political
lawyers in France.[1]   The influence of these scientist-politicians
was of late years not often on the side of liberty : the " intolerance of reason " so frequently conspicuous in the scientific
specialist, the impatience with the ways of the ordinary man so
characteristic of the expert, and the contempt for anything which
was not consciously organised by superior minds according to a
scientific blueprint, were phenomena familiar in German public
life for generations before they became of significance in this
country.   And perhaps no other country provides a better illustration of the effects on a nation of a general and thorough shift
of the greater part of its educational system from the " humanities " to the " realities " than Germany between 1840 and 1940.[2]

The way in which, in the end, with few exceptions, her scholars
and scientists put themselves readily at the service of the new
rulers is one of the most depressing and shameful spectacles in

[1] Cf. Franz Schnabel, *Deutsche Geschichte im neunzehnten Jahrhundert*, vol. II,
1933, p. 204.
[2] I believe it was the author of *Leviathan* who first suggested that the
teaching of the classics should be suppressed, because it instilled a dangerous
spirit of liberty !

the whole history of the rise of National-Socialism.[1] It is well known that particularly the scientists and engineers, who had so loudly claimed to be the leaders on the march to a new and better world, submitted more readily than almost any other class to the new tyranny.[2]

The rôle which the intellectuals played in the totalitarian transformation of society was prophetically foreseen in another country by Julien Benda, whose *Trahison des Clercs* assumes new significance when one now re-reads it, fifteen years after it has been written. There is particularly one passage in that work which deserves to be well pondered and kept in mind when we come to consider certain examples of the excursions of British scientists into politics. It is the passage in which M. Benda speaks of the

> superstition of science held to be competent in all domains, including that of morality ; a superstition which, I repeat, is an acquisition of the nineteenth century. It remains to discover whether those who brandish this doctrine believe in it or whether they simply want to give the prestige of a scientific appearance to passions of their hearts, which they perfectly know are nothing but passions. It is to be noted that the dogma that history is obedient to scientific laws is preached especially by partisans of arbitrary authority. This is quite natural, since it eliminates the two realities they most hate, i.e. human liberty and the historical action of the individual.

We have already had occasion to mention one English product of this kind, a work in which, on a Marxist background, all the

[1] The servility of the scientists to the powers that be appeared early in Germany, hand in hand with the great development of state-organised science which to-day is the subject of so much eulogy in this country. One of the most famous of German scientists, the physiologist Emil du Bois-Reymond, was not ashamed, in an oration delivered in 1870 in his double capacity of Rector of the University of Berlin and President of the Prussian Academy of Science, to proclaim that " We, the University of Berlin, quartered opposite the King's palace, are, by the deed of our foundation, the intellectual bodyguard of the House of Hohenzollern." (*A Speech on the German War*, London 1870, p. 31.—It is remarkable that du Bois-Reymond should have thought it advisable to issue an English edition of this oration.)

[2] It will suffice to quote one foreign witness : Mr. R. A. Brady, in his study of *The Spirit and Structure of German Fascism*, concludes his detailed account of the development in the German academic world with the statement that " the scientist, *per se*, is hence, perhaps, the most easily used and ' co-ordinated ' of all the especially trained people in modern society. The Nazis, to be true, fired a good many University professors, and dismissed a good many scientists from research laboratories. But the professors were primarily among the social sciences where there was more common awareness of and a more persistent criticism of the Nazi programmes, and not among the natural sciences where thinking is supposed to be most rigorous. Those dismissed in this latter field were primarily Jewish or exceptions to the generalisations made above, because of the equally uncritical acceptance of beliefs running contrary to Nazi views.—Consequently the Nazis were able to ' co-ordinate ' scholars and scientists with relative ease, and hence to throw behind their elaborate propaganda the seeming weight of the bulk of German learned opinion and support."

characteristic idiosyncrasies of the totalitarian intellectual, a hatred of almost everything which distinguishes European civilisation since the Renaissance, is combined with an approval of the methods of Inquisition. We do not wish to consider here such an extreme case and shall take a work which is more representative and which has achieved considerable publicity. Dr. C. H. Waddington's little book under the characteristic title *The Scientific Attitude* is as good an example as any of a class of literature which is actively sponsored by the influential weekly *Nature* and which combines claims for greater political power for the scientists with an ardent advocacy of wholesale " planning ". Though not quite as outspoken in his contempt for freedom as Mr. Crowther, Dr. Waddington is hardly more reassuring. He differs from most of the writers of the same kind in that he clearly sees and even emphasises that the tendencies he describes and supports inevitably lead to a totalitarian system. Yet apparently this appears to him preferable to what he describes as " the present ferocious monkey-house civilisation ".

Dr. Waddington's claim that the scientist is qualified to run a totalitarian society is based mainly on his thesis that " science can pass ethical judgment on human behaviour ", a claim to the elaboration of which by Dr. Waddington *Nature* has given considerable publicity. It is, of course, a thesis which has long been familiar to the German scientist-politicians and which has justly been singled out by J. Benda. For an illustration of what this means we do not need to go outside Dr. Waddington's book. Freedom, he explains, " is a very troublesome concept for the scientist to discuss, partly because he is not convinced that, in the last analysis, there is such a thing ". Nevertheless we are told that " science recognises " this and that kind of freedom, but " the freedom to be odd and unlike one's neighbour is not . . . a scientific value ". Apparently the " harlot humanities ", about which Dr. Waddington has to say many uncomplimentary things, have gravely misled us in teaching us tolerance !

That when it comes to social and economic questions this book on the " scientific attitude " is anything but scientific is what one has learnt to expect of this kind of literature. We find again all the familiar clichés and baseless generalisations about " potential plenty " and the inevitable tendency towards monopoly, though the " best authorities " quoted in support of these contentions prove on examination to be mostly political tracts of questionable scientific standing, while the serious studies of the same problems are conspicuously neglected.

As in almost all works of this type, Dr. Waddington's convictions are largely determined by his belief in " inevitable historical tendencies " which science is presumed to have discovered and which he derives from " the profound scientific philosophy " of Marxism whose basic notions are " almost, if not quite, identical with those underlying the scientific approach to nature " and which his " competence to judge " tells Dr. Waddington are an advance on anything which has gone before.   Thus Dr. Waddington, though he finds it " difficult to deny that England now is a worse country to live in than it was " in 1913, looks forward to an economic system which " will be centralised and totalitarian in the sense that all aspects of the economic development of large regions are consciously planned as an integrated whole ".   And for his facile optimism that in this totalitarian system freedom of thought will be preserved, his " scientific attitude " has no better counsel than the conviction that " there must be very valuable evidence about questions which one does not need to be an expert to understand ", such as, for example, whether it is possible " to combine totalitarianism with freedom of thought ".

*   *   *   *   *

A fuller survey of the various tendencies towards totalitarianism in this country would have to give considerable attention to the various attempts to create some kind of middle-class socialism bearing no doubt unknown to their authors an alarming resemblance to similar developments in pre-Hitler Germany.[1]   If we were concerned here with political movements proper we should have to consider such new organisations as the " Forward March " or " Common Wealth " movement of Sir Richard Acland, the author of *Unser Kampf*, or the activities of the " 1941 Committee " of Mr. J. B. Priestley, at one time associated with the former. But, though it would be unwise to disregard the symptomatic significance of such phenomena as these, they can hardly yet be counted as important political forces.   Apart from the intellectual influences which we have illustrated by two instances, the impetus of the movement towards totalitarianism comes mainly from the two great vested interests, organised capital and organised labour. Probably the greatest menace of all is the fact that the policies of these two most powerful groups point in the same direction. They do this through their common, and often concerted,

---

[1] Another element which after this war is likely to strengthen the tendencies in this direction will be some of the men who during the war have tasted the powers of coercive control and will find it difficult to reconcile themselves with the humbler rôles they will then have to play.   Though after the last war men of this kind were not as numerous as they will probably be in the future, they exercised even then a not inconsiderable influence on the economic policy of this country.   It was in the company of some of these men that as long as ten or twelve years ago I first experienced in this country the then still unusual sensation of being suddenly transported into what I had learnt to regard as a thoroughly " German " intellectual atmosphere.

support of the monopolistic organisation of industry ; and it is this tendency which is the great immediate danger. While there is no reason to believe that this movement is inevitable, there can be little doubt that if we continue on the path we have been treading, it will lead us to totalitarianism.

This movement is, of course, deliberately planned mainly by the capitalist organisers of monopolies, and they are thus one of the main sources of this danger. Their responsibility is not altered by the fact that their aim is not a totalitarian system but rather a sort of corporative society in which the organised industries would appear as semi-independent and self-governing " estates ". But they are as short-sighted as were their German colleagues in believing that they will be allowed not only to create but also for any length of time to run such a system. The decisions which the managers of such an organised industry would constantly have to make are not decisions which any society will long leave to private individuals. A state which allows such enormous aggregations of power to grow up cannot afford to let this power rest entirely in private control. Nor is the belief any less illusory that in such conditions the entrepreneurs will be long allowed to enjoy the favoured position which in a competitive society is justified by the fact that of the many who take the risks only a few achieve the success the chances of which make the risk worth taking. It is not surprising that entrepreneurs should like to enjoy both the high income which in a competitive society the successful ones among them gain, and the security of the civil servant. So long as a large sector of private industry exists side by side with the government-run industry great industrial talent is likely to command high salaries even in fairly secure positions. But while the entrepreneurs may well see their expectations borne out during a transition stage, it will not be long before they will find, as their German colleagues did, that they are no longer masters but will in every respect have to be satisfied with whatever power and emoluments the government will concede them.

Unless the argument of this book has been completely misunderstood, the author will not be suspected of any tenderness towards the capitalists if he stresses here that it would nevertheless be a mistake to put the blame for the modern movement towards monopoly exclusively or mainly on that class. Their propensity in this direction is neither new nor would it by itself be likely to become a formidable power. The fatal development was that they have succeeded in enlisting the support of an ever-increasing number of other groups and with their help to obtain the support of the state.

In some measure the monopolists have gained this support

either by letting other groups participate in their gains or, and perhaps even more frequently, by persuading them that the formation of monopolies was in the public interest. But the change in public opinion which through its influence on legislation and judicature [1] has been the most important factor to make this development possible, is more than anything the result of the propaganda against competition by the Left. Very frequently even measures aimed against the monopolists in fact serve only to strengthen the power of monopoly. Every raid on the gains of monopoly, be it in the interest of particular groups or of the state as a whole, tends to create new vested interests which will help to bolster up monopoly. A system in which large privileged groups profit from the gains of monopoly may be politically much more dangerous, and monopoly in such a system certainly is much more powerful, than in one where the profits go to a limited few. But though it should be clear that, for example, the higher wages which the monopolist is in a position to pay are just as much the result of exploitation as his own profit, and are just as certain to make poorer not only all the consumers but still more all other wage earners, not merely those who benefit from it but the public generally nowadays accept the ability to pay higher wages as a legitimate argument in favour of monopoly.[2]

There is serious reason for doubt whether even in those cases where monopoly is inevitable the best way of controlling it is to put it in the hands of the state. If only a single industry were in question this might well be so. But when we have to deal with many different monopolistic industries, there is much to be said for leaving them in different private hands rather than combining them under the single control of the state. Even if railways, road and air transport, or the supply of gas and electricity, were all inevitably monopolies, the consumer is unquestionably in a much stronger position so long as they remain separate monopolies than when they are " co-ordinated " by a central control. Private monopoly is scarcely ever complete and even more rarely of long duration or able to disregard potential competition. But a state monopoly is always a state-protected monopoly—protected against both potential competition and effective criticism.

[1] Cf. on this the recent instructive article on " Monopoly and the Law ", by W. Arthur Lewis, in *The Modern Law Review*, vol. VI, no. 3, April 1943.
[2] Even more surprising, perhaps, is the remarkable tenderness which many socialists are apt to show towards the *rentier* bondholder to whom monopolist organisation of industry frequently guarantees secure incomes. That their blind enmity to profits should lead people to represent effortless fixed income as socially or ethically more desirable than profits, and to accept even monopoly to secure such a guaranteed income to, for example, railway bondholders, is one of the most extraordinary symptoms of the perversion of values which has taken place during the last generation.

It means in most instances that a temporary monopoly is given the power to secure its position for all time—a power almost certain to be used. Where the power which ought to check and control monopoly becomes interested in sheltering and defending its appointees, where for the government to remedy an abuse is to admit responsibility for it, and where criticism of the actions of monopoly means criticism of the government, there is little hope of monopoly becoming the servant of the community. A state which is entangled in all directions in the running of monopolistic enterprise, while it would possess crushing power over the individual, would yet be a weak state in so far as its freedom in formulating policy is concerned. The machinery of monopoly becomes identical with the machinery of the state, and the state itself becomes more and more identified with the interests of those who run things than with the interests of the people in general.

The probability is that wherever monopoly is really inevitable the plan which used to be preferred by the Americans, of a strong state control over private monopolies, if consistently pursued, offers a better chance of satisfactory results than state management. This would at least seem to be so where the state enforces a stringent price control which leaves no room for extraordinary profits in which others than the monopolists can participate. Even if this should have the effect (as it sometimes had with American public utilities) that the services of the monopolistic industries would become less satisfactory than they might be, this would be a small price to pay for an effective check on the powers of monopoly. Personally I should much prefer to have to put up with some such inefficiency than have organised monopoly control my ways of life. Such a method of dealing with monopoly, which would rapidly make the position of the monopolist the least eligible among entrepreneurial positions, would also do as much as anything to reduce monopoly to the spheres where it is inevitable and to stimulate the invention of substitutes which can be provided competitively. Only make the position of the monopolist once more that of the whipping boy of economic policy and you will be surprised how quickly most of the abler entrepreneurs will rediscover their taste for the bracing air of competition!

* * * * *

The problem of monopoly would not be as difficult as it is if it were only the capitalist monopolist whom we have to fight. But, as has already been said, monopoly has become the danger that it is, not through the efforts of a few interested capitalists, but through the support they have obtained from those whom they have let share in their gains, and from the many more whom they have persuaded that in supporting monopoly they assist in the creation of a more just and orderly society. The fatal turning point in the modern development was when the great movement which can serve its original ends only by fighting all privilege, the Labour Movement, came under the influence of anti-competition doctrines and became itself entangled in the strife for privilege. The recent growth of monopoly is largely the result of a deliberate collaboration of organised capital and organised labour where the privileged groups of labour share in the monopoly profits at the expense of the community and particularly at the expense of the poorest, those employed in the less well organised industries and the unemployed.

It is one of the saddest spectacles of our time to see a great democratic movement support a policy which must lead to the destruction of democracy and which meanwhile can benefit only a minority of the masses who support it. Yet it is this support from the Left of the tendencies towards monopoly which make them so irresistible and the prospects of the future so dark. So long as Labour continues to assist in the destruction of the only order under which at least some degree of independence and freedom has been secured to every worker, there is indeed little hope for the future. The Labour leaders who now proclaim so loudly that they have " done once and for all with the mad competitive system " [1] are proclaiming the doom of the freedom of the individual. There is no other possibility than either the order governed by the impersonal discipline of the market or that directed by the will of a few individuals ; and those who are out to destroy the first are wittingly or unwittingly helping to create the second. Even though some workmen will perhaps be better fed, and all will no doubt be more uniformly dressed in that new order, it is permissible to doubt whether the majority of English workmen will in the end thank the intellectuals among their leaders who have presented them with a socialist doctrine which endangers their personal freedom.

To anyone who is familiar with the history of the major Continental countries in the last twenty-five years, the study of the recent programme of the Labour Party, now committed to the creation of a " planned society " is a most depressing experience. To " any attempt to restore traditional Britain " there is opposed a scheme which not only in general outline but also in detail and even wording is indistinguishable from the socialist dreams

[1] Professor H. J. Laski, in his address to the 41st Annual Labour Party Conference, London, May 26, 1942 (*Report*, p. 111). It deserves to be noted that according to Professor Laski it is " this mad competitive system which spells poverty for all peoples, and war as outcome of that poverty "—a curious reading of the history of the last hundred and fifty years.

which dominated German discussion twenty-five years ago. Not only demands, like those of the resolution, adopted on Professor Laski's motion, which requires the retention in peace time of the " measures of Government control needed for mobilising the national resources in war ", but all the characteristic catchwords, such as the " balanced economy " which Professor Laski now demands for Great Britain, or the " community consumption " towards which production is to be centrally directed, are bodily taken over from the German ideology.   Twenty-five years ago there was perhaps still some excuse for holding the naïve belief " that a planned society can be a far more free society than the competitive *laissez-faire* order it has come to replace ".[1] But to find it once more held after twenty-five years of experience and the re-examination of the old beliefs to which this experience has led, and at a time when we are fighting the results of those very doctrines, is tragic beyond words.   That the great party which in Parliament and public opinion has largely taken the place of the progressive parties of the past, should have ranged itself with what, in the light of all past development, must be regarded as a reactionary movement, is the decisive change which has taken place in our time and the source of the mortal danger to everything a liberal must value.   That the advances of the past should be threatened by the traditionalist forces of the Right is a phenomenon of all ages which need not alarm us.   But if the place of the opposition, in public discussion as well as in Parliament, should become lastingly the monopoly of a second reactionary party, there would indeed be no hope left.

[1] *The Old World and the New Society*, an Interim Report of the National Executive of the British Labour Party on the Problems of Reconstruction, pp. 12 and 16.

CHAPTER XIV

MATERIAL CONDITIONS AND IDEAL ENDS

> Is it just or reasonable, that most voices against the main end
> of government should enslave the less number that would be
> free ? More just it is, doubtless, if it come to force, that a less
> number compel a greater to retain, which can be no wrong to
> them, their liberty, than that a greater number, for the pleasure
> of their baseness, compel a less most injuriously to be their
> fellow slaves. They who seek nothing but their own just
> liberty, have always the right to win it, whenever they have the
> power, be the voices never so numerous that oppose it.
>
> *John Milton.*

OUR generation likes to flatter itself that it attaches less weight
to economic considerations than did its parents or grandparents.
The " End of Economic Man " bids fair to become one of the
governing myths of our age. Before we accept this claim, or
treat the change as praiseworthy, we must inquire a little further
how far it is true. When we consider the claims for social reconstruction which are most strongly pressed it appears that they are
almost all economic in character : we have seen already that the
" re-interpretation in economic terms " of the political ideals of
the past, of liberty, equality, and security, is one of the main
demands of people who at the same time proclaim the end of
economic man. Nor can there be much doubt that in their
beliefs and aspirations men are to-day more than ever before
governed by economic doctrines, by the carefully fostered belief
in the irrationality of our economic system, by the false assertions
about " potential plenty ", pseudo-theories about the inevitable
trend towards monopoly, and the impression created by certain
much advertised occurrences such as the destruction of stocks
of raw materials or the suppression of inventions, for which
competition is blamed, though they are precisely the sort of
thing which could not happen under competition and which are
made possible only by monopoly and usually by government-
aided monopoly.[1]

In a different sense, however, it is no doubt true that our

---

[1] The frequent use that is made of the occasional destruction of wheat, coffee,
etc:, as an argument against competition is a good illustration of the intellectual
dishonesty of much of this argument, since a little reflection will show that in
a competitive market no owner of such stocks can gain by their destruction.
The case of the alleged suppression of useful patents is more complicated and
cannot be adequately discussed in a note ; but the conditions in which it would
be profitable to put into cold storage a patent *which in the social interest ought
to be used* are so exceptional that it is more than doubtful whether this has
happened in any important instance.

generation is less willing to listen to economic considerations than was true of its predecessors. It is most decidedly unwilling to sacrifice any of its demands to what are called economic arguments, it is impatient and intolerant of all restraints on their immediate ambitions, and unwilling to bow to economic necessities. It is not any contempt for material welfare, or even any diminished desire for it, but, on the contrary, a refusal to recognise any obstacles, any conflict with other aims which might impede the fulfilment of their own desires, which distinguishes our generation. Economophobia would be a more correct description of this attitude than the doubly misleading " End of Economic Man ", which suggests a change from a state of affairs which has never existed in a direction in which we are not moving. Man has come to hate, and to revolt against, the impersonal forces to which in the past he submitted even though they have often frustrated his individual efforts.

This revolt is an instance of a much more general phenomenon, a new unwillingness to submit to any rule or necessity the *rationale* of which man does not understand ; it makes itself felt in many fields of life, particularly in that of morals ; and it is often a commendable attitude. But there are fields where this craving for intelligibility cannot be fully satisfied and where at the same time a refusal to submit to anything we cannot understand must lead to the destruction of our civilisation. Though it is natural that, as the world around us becomes more complex, our resistance grows against the forces which, without our understanding them, constantly interfere with individual hopes and plans, it is just in these circumstances that it becomes less and less possible for anyone fully to understand these forces. A complex civilisation like ours is necessarily based on the individual adjusting himself to changes whose cause and nature he cannot understand : why he should have more or less, why he should have to move to another occupation, why some things he wants should become more difficult to get than others, will always be connected with such a multitude of circumstances that no single mind will be able to grasp them ; or, even worse, those affected will put all the blame on an obvious immediate and avoidable cause, while the more complex interrelationships which determine the change remain inevitably hidden to them. Even the director of a completely planned society, if he wanted to give an adequate explanation to anyone why he has to be directed to a different job, or why his remuneration has to be changed, could not fully do so without explaining and vindicating his whole plan—which means, of course, that it could not be explained to more than a few.

It was men's submission to the impersonal forces of the market that in the past has made possible the growth of a civilisation which without this could not have developed ; it is by thus submitting that we are every day helping to build something that is greater than anyone of us can fully comprehend. It does not matter whether men in the past did submit from beliefs which some now regard as superstitious : from a religious spirit of humility, or an exaggerated respect for the crude teachings of the early economists. The crucial point is that it is infinitely more difficult rationally to comprehend the necessity of submitting to forces whose operation we cannot follow in detail, than to do so out of the humble awe which religion, or even the respect for the doctrines of economics, did inspire. It may indeed be the case that infinitely more intelligence on the part of everybody would be needed than anybody now possesses, if we were even merely to maintain our present complex civilisation without anybody having to do things of which he does not comprehend the necessity. The refusal to yield to forces which we neither understand nor can recognise as the conscious decisions of an intelligent being is the product of an incomplete and therefore erroneous rationalism. It is incomplete because it fails to comprehend that the co-ordination of the multifarious individual efforts in a complex society must take account of facts no individual can completely survey. And it fails to see that, unless this complex society is to be destroyed, the only alternative to submission to the impersonal and seemingly irrational forces of the market is submission to an equally uncontrollable and therefore arbitrary power of other men. In his anxiety to escape the irksome restraints which he now feels, man does not realise that the new authoritarian restraints which will have to be deliberately imposed in their stead will be even more painful.

Those who argue that we have to an astounding degree learned to master the forces of nature but are sadly behind in making successful use of the possibilities of social collaboration are quite right so far as this statement goes. But they are mistaken when they carry the comparison further and argue that we must learn to master the forces of society in the same manner in which we have learnt to master the forces of nature. This is not only the path to totalitarianism, but the path to the destruction of our civilisation and a certain way to block future progress. Those who demand it show by their very demands that they have not yet comprehended the extent to which the mere preservation of what we have so far achieved depends on the co-ordination of individual efforts by impersonal forces.

*   *   *   *   *

We must now return briefly to the crucial point, that individual freedom cannot be reconciled with the supremacy of one single purpose to which the whole society must be entirely and permanently subordinated.   The only exception to the rule that a free society must not be subjected to a single purpose is war and other temporary disasters when subordination of almost everything to the immediate and pressing need is the price at which we preserve our freedom in the long run.   This explains also why so many of the fashionable phrases about doing for the purposes of peace what we have learnt to do for the purposes of war are so very misleading : it is sensible temporarily to sacrifice freedom in order to make it more secure in the future ; but the same cannot be said for a system proposed as a permanent arrangement.

That no single purpose must be allowed in peace to have absolute preference over all others applies even to the one aim which everybody now agrees comes in the front rank : the conquest of unemployment.   There can be no doubt that this must be the goal of our greatest endeavour ; even so, it does not mean that such an aim should be allowed to dominate us to the exclusion of everything else, that, as the glib phrase runs, it must be accomplished " at any price ".   It is, in fact, in this field that the fascination of vague but popular phrases like " full employment " may well lead to extremely short-sighted measures, and where the categorical and irresponsible " it must be done at all cost " of the single-minded idealist is likely to do the greatest harm.

It is of very great importance that we should approach with open eyes the task which in this field we shall have to face after the war, and that we should clearly realise what we may hope to achieve.   One of the dominant features of the immediate post-war situation will be that the special needs of war have drawn hundreds of thousands of men and women into specialised jobs where during the war they have been able to earn relatively high wages. There will, in many instances, be no possibility of employing the same numbers in these particular trades.   There will be an urgent need for the transfer of large numbers to other jobs, and many of them will find that the work they can then get is less favourably remunerated than was true of their war job.   Even re-training, which certainly ought to be provided on a liberal scale, cannot entirely overcome this problem.   There will still be many people who, if they are to be paid according to what their services will then be worth to society, would under any system have to be content with a lowering of their material position relative to that of others.

If, then, the trade unions successfully resist any lowering of the wages of the particular groups in question, there will be only two alternatives open : either coercion will have to be used, i.e. certain individuals will have to be selected for compulsory transfer to other and relatively less well paid positions, or those who can no longer be employed at the relatively high wages they have earned during the war must be allowed to remain unemployed till they are willing to accept work at a relatively lower wage. This is a problem which would arise in a socialist society no less than in any other ; and the great majority of workmen would probably be just as little inclined to guarantee in perpetuity their present wages to those who were drawn into specially well paid employments because of the special need of war. A socialist society would certainly use coercion in this position. The point that is relevant for us is that if we are determined not to allow unemployment at any price, and are not willing to use coercion, we shall be driven to all sorts of desperate expedients, none of which can bring any lasting relief and all of which will seriously interfere with the most productive use of our resources. It should be specially noted that monetary policy cannot provide a real cure for this difficulty except by a general and considerable inflation, sufficient to raise all other wages and prices relatively to those which cannot be lowered, and that even this would bring about the desired result only by effecting in a concealed and underhand fashion that reduction of real wages which could not be brought about directly. Yet to raise all other wages and incomes to an extent sufficient to adjust the position of the group in question would involve an inflationary expansion on such a scale that the disturbances, hardships, and injustices caused would be much greater than those to be cured.

This problem, which will arise in a particularly acute form after the war, is one which will always be with us so long as the economic system has to adapt itself to continuous changes. There will always be a possible maximum of employment in the short run which can be achieved by giving all people employment where they happen to be and which can be achieved by monetary expansion. But not only can this maximum be maintained solely by progressive inflationary expansion and with the effect of holding up those redistributions of labour between industries made necessary by the changed circumstances, and which so long as workmen are free to choose their jobs will always come about only with some delays and thereby cause some unemployment: to aim always at the maximum of employment achievable by monetary means is a policy which is certain in the end to defeat its own purposes. It tends to lower the productivity of labour and thereby constantly increases the proportion of the working population which can be kept employed at present wages only by artificial means.

* * * * *

There is little doubt that after the war wisdom in the management of our economic affairs will be even more important than before and that the fate of our civilisation will ultimately depend on how we solve the economic problems we shall then face. We shall at first be poor, very poor indeed—and the problem of regaining and improving our former standards may in fact prove for Great Britain more difficult than for many other countries. If we act wisely there is little question that by hard work and by devoting a considerable part of our efforts to overhauling and renewing our industrial apparatus and organisation, we shall in the course of a few years be able to return to, and even to surpass, the level we had reached. But this presupposes that we shall be satisfied to consume currently no more than is possible without impairing the task of reconstruction, that no exaggerated hopes create irresistible claims for more than this, and that we regard it as more important to use our resources in the best manner and for the purposes where they contribute most to our well-being than that we should use all our resources somehow.[1] Perhaps no less important is that we should not, by short-sighted attempts to cure poverty by a redistribution instead of by an increase in our income, so depress large classes as to turn them into determined enemies of the existing political order. It should never be forgotten that the one decisive factor in the rise of totalitarianism on the Continent, which is yet absent in this country, is the existence of a large recently dispossessed middle class.

Our hopes of avoiding the fate which threatens must indeed to a large extent rest on the prospect that we can resume rapid economic progress which, however low we may have to start, will continue to carry us upwards ; and the main condition for such progress is that we should all be ready to adapt ourselves quickly to a very much changed world, that no considerations for the accustomed standard of particular groups must be allowed to obstruct this adaptation, and that we learn once more to turn all our resources to wherever they contribute most to make us all richer. The adjustments that will be needed if we are to recover and surpass our former standards will be greater than any similar adjustments we had to make in the past ; and only if every one of us is ready individually to obey the necessities of this readjustment shall we be able to get through a difficult period as free

---

[1] This is perhaps the place to emphasise that, however much one may wish a speedy return to a free economy, this cannot mean the removal at one stroke of most of the wartime restrictions. Nothing would discredit the system of free enterprise more than the acute, though probably short-lived, dislocation and instability such an attempt would produce. The problem is at what kind of system we should aim in the process of demobilisation, not whether the wartime system should be transformed into more permanent arrangements by a carefully thought-out policy of gradual relaxation of controls, which may have to extend over several years.

men who can choose their own way of life. Let a uniform minimum be secured to everybody by all means ; but let us admit at the same time that with this assurance of a basic minimum all claims for a privileged security of particular classes must lapse, that all excuses disappear for allowing groups to exclude new-comers from sharing their relative prosperity in order to maintain a special standard of their own.

It may sound noble to say : damn economics, let us build up a decent world—but it is, in fact, merely irresponsible. With our world as it is, with everyone convinced that the material conditions here or there must be improved, our only chance of building a decent world is that we can continue to improve the general level of wealth. The one thing modern democracy will not bear without cracking is the necessity of a substantial lowering of the standards of living in peace time or even prolonged stationariness of its economic conditions.

*　　*　　*　　*　　*

People who admit that present political trends constitute a serious threat to our economic prospects, and through their economic effects endanger much higher values, are yet apt to deceive themselves that we are making material sacrifices to gain ideal ends. It is, however, more than doubtful whether a fifty years' approach towards collectivism has raised our moral standards, or whether the change has not rather been in the opposite direction. Though we are in the habit of priding ourselves on our more sensitive social conscience, it is by no means clear that this is justified by the practice of our individual conduct. On the negative side, in its indignation about the inequities of the existing social order, our generation probably surpasses most of its predecessors. But the effect of that movement on our positive standards in the proper field of morals, individual conduct, and on the seriousness with which we uphold moral principles against the expediencies and exigencies of social machinery, is a very different matter.

Issues in this field have become so confused that it is necessary to go back to fundamentals. What our generation is in danger of forgetting is not only that morals are of necessity a phenomenon of individual conduct, but also that they can exist only in the sphere in which the individual is free to decide for himself and called upon voluntarily to sacrifice personal advantage to the observance of a moral rule. Outside the sphere of individual responsibility there is neither goodness nor badness, neither opportunity for moral merit nor the chance of proving one's con-viction by sacrificing one's desires to what one thinks right. Only where we ourselves are responsible for our own interests

and are free to sacrifice them, has our decision moral value. We
are neither entitled to be unselfish at someone else's expense, nor
is there any merit in being unselfish if we have no choice. The
members of a society who in all respects are *made* to do the good
thing have no title to praise. As Milton said : " If every action
which is good or evil in a man of ripe years were under pittance
and prescription and compulsion, what were virtue but a name,
what praise should then be due to well-doing, what gramercy
to be sober, just, or continent ? "

Freedom to order our own conduct in the sphere where material
circumstances force a choice upon us, and responsibility for the
arrangement of our own life according to our own conscience, is
the air in which alone moral sense grows and in which moral
values are daily re-created in the free decision of the individual.
Responsibility, not to a superior, but to one's conscience, the
awareness of a duty not exacted by compulsion, the necessity to
decide which of the things one values are to be sacrificed to others,
and to bear the consequences of one's own decision, are the very
essence of any morals which deserve the name.

That in this sphere of individual conduct the effect of col-
léctivism has been almost entirely destructive, is both inevitable
and undeniable. A movement whose main promise is the
relief from responsibility [1] cannot but be anti-moral in its effect,
however lofty the ideals to which it owes its birth. Can there be
much doubt that the feeling of personal obligation to remedy inequities, where our individual power permits, has been weakened
rather than strengthened, that both the willingness to bear
responsibility and the consciousness that it is our own individual
duty to know how to choose have been perceptibly impaired ?
There is all the difference between demanding that a desirable
state of affairs should be brought about by the authorities or
even being willing to submit provided everyone else is made to
do the same, and the readiness to do what one thinks right oneself
at the sacrifice of one's own desires and perhaps in the face of
hostile public opinion. There is much to suggest that we have

---

[1] This becomes more and more clearly expressed as socialism approaches
totalitarianism, and in this country is most explicitly stated in the programme
of that latest and most totalitarian form of English socialism, Sir Richard
Acland's " Common-Wealth " movement. The main feature of the new order
he promises is that in it the community will " say to the individual ' Don't *you*
bother about the business of getting your *own* living '." In consequence, of
course, " it must be the community as a whole which must decide whether or
not a man shall be employed upon our resources, and how and when and in
what manner he shall work ", and that the community will have " to run
camps for shirkers in very tolerable conditions ". Is it surprising that the
author discovers that Hitler " has stumbled across (or has needed to make use
of) a small part, or perhaps one should say one particular aspect of, what will
ultimately be required of humanity " ? (Sir Richard Acland, Bt., *The Forward
March*, 1941, pp. 127, 126, 135, and 32).

in fact become more tolerant towards particular abuses, and much more indifferent to inequities in individual cases, since we have fixed our eyes on an entirely different system in which the state will set everything right. It may even be, as has been suggested, that the passion for collective action is a way in which we now without compunction collectively indulge in that selfishness which as individuals we had learnt a little to restrain.

It is true that the virtues which are less esteemed and practised now—independence, self-reliance, and the willingness to bear risks, the readiness to back one's own conviction against a majority, and the willingness to voluntary co-operations with one's neighbours—are essentially those on which the working of an individualist society rests. Collectivism has nothing to put in their place, and in so far as it already has destroyed them it has left a void filled by nothing but the demand for obedience and the compulsion of the individual to do what is collectively decided to be good. The periodical election of representatives, to which the moral choice of the individual tends to be more and more reduced, is not an occasion on which his moral values are tested or where he has constantly to reassert and prove the order of his values, and to testify to the sincerity of his profession by the sacrifice of those of his values he rates lower to those he puts higher.

As the rules of conduct evolved by individuals are the source from which collective political action derives what moral standards it possesses, it would indeed be surprising if the relaxation of the standards of individual conduct were accompanied by a raising of the standards of social action. That there have been great changes is clear. Every generation, of course, puts some values higher and some lower than its predecessors. Which, however, are the aims which take a lower place now, which are the values which we are now warned may have to give way if they come into conflict with others ? Which kind of values figure less prominently in the picture of the future held out to us by the popular writers and speakers than they did in the dreams and hopes of our fathers ? It is certainly not material comfort, certainly not a rise in our standard of living or the assurance of a certain status in society which ranks lower. Is there a popular writer or speaker who dares to suggest to the masses that they might have to make sacrifices of their material prospects for the enhancement of an ideal end ? Is it not, in fact, entirely the other way round ? Are not the things which we are more and more frequently taught to regard as " nineteenth-century illusions " all moral values—liberty and independence, truth and intellectual honesty, peace and democracy, and the respect for the individual *qua* man instead of merely as the member of an organised group ? What are the fixed poles now which are regarded as sacrosanct, which no reformer dare touch, since they are treated as the immutable boundaries which must be respected in any plan for the future ?   They are no longer the liberty of the individual, his freedom of movement, and scarcely that of speech.   They are the protected standards of this or that group, their " right " to exclude others from providing their fellow-men with what they need.   Discrimination between members and non-members of closed groups, not to speak of nationals of different countries, is accepted more and more as a matter of course ;   injustices inflicted on individuals by government action in the interest of a group are disregarded with an indifference hardly distinguishable from callousness ;   and the grossest violations of the most elementary rights of the individual, such as are involved in the compulsory transfer of populations, are more and more often countenanced even by supposed liberals.   All this surely indicates that our moral sense has been blunted rather than sharpened.   When we are reminded, as more and more frequently happens, that one cannot make omelettes without breaking eggs, the eggs which are broken are almost all of the kind which a generation or two ago were regarded as the essential bases of civilised life.   And what atrocities committed by powers with whose professed principles they sympathise have not been readily condoned by many of our so-called " liberals " ?

*   *   *   *   *

There is one aspect of the change in moral values brought about by the advance of collectivism which at the present time provides special food for thought.   It is that the virtues which are held less and less in esteem and which consequently become rarer are precisely those on which the British people justly prided themselves and in which they were generally recognised to excel.   The virtues possessed by the British people possessed in a higher degree than most other people, excepting only a few of the smaller nations, like the Swiss and the Dutch, were independence and self-reliance, individual initiative and local responsibility, the successful reliance on voluntary activity, non-interference with one's neighbour and tolerance of the different and queer, respect for custom and tradition, and a healthy suspicion of power and authority.   British strength, British character, and British achievements are to a great extent the result of a cultivation of the spontaneous.   But almost all the traditions and institutions in which British moral genius has found its most characteristic expression, and which in turn have moulded the national character and the whole moral climate of England, are those which the progress of collectivism and its inherently centralistic tendencies are progressively destroying.

A foreign background is sometimes helpful in seeing more clearly to what circumstances the peculiar excellencies of the moral atmosphere of a nation are due.   And if one who, whatever the law may say, must for ever remain a foreigner, may be allowed to say so, it is one of the most disheartening spectacles of our time to see to what extent some of the most precious things which England has given to the world are now held in contempt in England herself.   The English hardly know to what degree they differ from most other people in that they all, irrespective of party, hold to a greater or less extent the ideas which in their most pronounced form are known as liberalism.   Compared with most other peoples only twenty years ago almost all Englishmen were liberals—however much they may have differed from party Liberalism.   And even to-day the English conservative or socialist, no less than the liberal, if he travels abroad, though he may find the ideas and writings of Carlyle or Disraeli, of the Webbs or H. G. Wells, exceedingly popular in circles with which he has little in common, among Nazis and other totalitarians, if he finds an intellectual island where the tradition of Macaulay and Gladstone, of J. S. Mill or John Morley lives, will find kindred spirits who " talk the same language " as himself—however much he himself may differ from the ideals for which these men specifically stood.

Nowhere is the loss of the belief in the specific values of British civilisation more manifest, and nowhere has it had a more paralysing effect on the pursuit of our immediate great purpose than in the fatuous ineffectiveness of most British propaganda. The first prerequisite for success in propaganda directed to other people is the proud acknowledgment of the characteristic values and distinguishing traits for which the country attempting it is known to the other peoples.   The main cause of the ineffectiveness of British propaganda is that those directing it seem to have lost their own belief in the peculiar values of English civilisation or to be completely ignorant of the main points on which it differs from that of other people.   The Left intelligentsia, indeed, have so long worshipped foreign gods that they seem to have become almost incapable of seeing any good in the characteristic English institutions and traditions.   That the moral values on which most of them pride themselves are largely the product of the institutions they are out to destroy, these socialists cannot, of course, admit.   And this attitude is unfortunately not confined to avowed socialists.   Though one must hope that this is not true of the less vocal but more numerous cultivated Englishmen, if one were to judge by the ideas which find expression in current political discussion and propaganda the Englishmen who not only " the language speak that Shakespeare spake ", but also " the faith and morals hold that Milton held " seem to have almost vanished.[1]

To believe, however, that the kind of propaganda produced by this attitude can have the desired effect on our enemies and particularly the Germans, is a fatal blunder. The Germans know this country, not well, perhaps, yet sufficiently to know what are the characteristic traditional values of British life, and what for the past two or three generations has increasingly separated the minds of the two countries. If we wish to convince them, not only of our sincerity, but also that we have to offer a real alternative to the way they have gone, it will not be by concessions to their system of thought. We shall not delude them with a stale reproduction of the ideas of their fathers which we have borrowed from them—be it state-socialism, " Realpolitik ", " scientific " planning, or corporativism. We shall not persuade them by following them half the way which leads to totalitarianism. If the English themselves abandon the supreme ideal of the freedom and happiness of the individual, if they implicitly admit that their civilisation is not worth preserving, and that they know nothing better than to follow the path along which the Germans have led, they have indeed nothing to offer. To the Germans all these are merely belated admissions that the British have been wrong all the way through, and that they themselves are leading the way to a new and better world, however appalling the period of transition may be. The Germans know that what they still regard as the British tradition and their own new ideals are fundamentally opposed and irreconcilable views of life. They might be convinced that the way they have chosen was wrong—but nothing will ever convince them that the British will be better guides on the German path.

Least of all will that type of propaganda appeal to those Germans on whose help we must ultimately count in rebuilding Europe because their values are nearest to our own. For experience has made them wiser and sadder men : they have learnt that neither good intentions nor efficiency of organisation can preserve decency in a system in which personal freedom and individual responsibility are destroyed. What the German and Italian who have learned the lesson above all want is protection against the monster state—not grandiose schemes for organisation on a colossal scale, but opportunity peacefully and in freedom to build

---

[1] Though the subject of this chapter has already invited more than one reference to Milton, it is difficult to resist the temptation to add here one more quotation, a very familiar one, though one, it seems, which nowadays nobody but a foreigner would dare to cite : " Let not England forget her precedence of teaching nations how to live." It is, perhaps, significant that our generation has seen a host of American and English detractors of Milton—and that the first of them, Mr. Ezra Pound, was during this war broadcasting from Italy !

up once more his own little world.   It is not because they believe
that to be ordered about by the British is preferable to being
ordered about by the Prussians, but because they believe that in
a world where British ideals have been victorious they will be
less ordered about and left in peace to pursue their own concerns,
that we can hope for support from some of the nationals of the
enemy countries.

If we are to succeed in the war of ideologies and to win over
the decent elements in the enemy countries, we must first of all
regain the belief in the traditional values for which this country
stood in the past, and must have the moral courage stoutly to
defend the ideals which our enemies attack.   Not by shamefaced
apologies and by assurances that we are rapidly reforming, not
by explaining that we are seeking some compromise between the
traditional English values and the new totalitarian ideas, shall we
win confidence and support.   Not the latest improvements we
may have effected in our social institutions, which count but little
compared with the basic differences of two opposed ways of life,
but our unwavering faith in those traditions which have made
this country a country of free and upright, tolerant and independent people, is the thing that counts.

CHAPTER XV

THE PROSPECTS OF INTERNATIONAL ORDER

> Of all checks on democracy, federation has been the most
> efficacious and the most congenial. . . . The federal system
> limits and restrains the sovereign power by dividing it and by
> assigning to Government only certain defined rights. It is
> the only method of curbing not only the majority but the
> power of the whole people. *Lord Acton.*

IN no other field has the world yet paid so dearly for the abandonment of nineteenth-century liberalism as in the field where the
retreat began : in international relations. Yet only a small part
of the lesson which experience ought to have taught us has been
learnt. Perhaps even more than elsewhere current notions of
what is desirable and practicable are here still of a kind which
may well produce the opposite of what they promise.

The part of the lesson of the recent past which is slowly and
gradually being appreciated is that many kinds of economic
planning, conducted independently on a national scale, are bound
in their aggregate effect to be harmful even from a purely economic
point of view, and in addition to produce serious international
friction. That there is little hope of international order or lasting
peace so long as every country is free to employ whatever measures
it thinks desirable in its own immediate interest, however
damaging they may be to others, needs little emphasis now.
Many kinds of economic planning are indeed practicable only if
the planning authority can effectively shut out all extraneous
influences ; the result of such planning is therefore inevitably the
piling up of restrictions on the movements of men and goods.

Less obvious but by no means less real are the dangers to peace
arising out of the artificially fostered economic solidarity of all
the inhabitants of any one country, and from the new blocks
of opposed interests created by planning on a national scale. It
is neither necessary nor desirable that national boundaries
should mark sharp differences in standards of living, that membership of a national group should entitle to a share in a cake
altogether different from that in which members of other groups
share. If the resources of different nations are treated as
exclusive properties of these nations as wholes, if international
economic relations, instead of being relations between individuals,
become increasingly relations between whole nations organised as
trading bodies, they inevitably become the source of friction and
envy between whole nations. It is one of the most fatal illusions

that by substituting negotiations between states or organised groups for competition for markets or for raw materials, international friction would be reduced. This would merely put a contest of force in the place of what can only metaphorically be called the " struggle " of competition, and transfer to powerful and armed states, subject to no superior law, the rivalries which between individuals had to be decided without recourse to force. Economic transactions between national bodies who are at the same time the supreme judges of their own behaviour, who bow to no superior law, and whose representatives cannot be bound by any considerations but the immediate interest of their respective nations, must end in clashes of power.[1]

If we were to make no better use of victory than to countenance existing trends in this direction, only too visible before 1939, we might indeed find that we have defeated National-Socialism merely to create a world of many national socialisms, differing in detail, but all equally totalitarian, nationalistic, and in recurrent conflict with each other. The Germans would appear as the disturbers of peace, as they already do to some people,[2] merely because they were the first to take the path along which all the others were ultimately to follow.

*　　*　　*　　*　　*

Those who at least partly realise these dangers usually draw the conclusion that economic planning must be done " internationally ", i.e. by some super-national authority. But though this would avert some of the obvious dangers raised by planning on a national scale, it seems that those who advocate such ambitious schemes have little conception of the even greater difficulties and dangers which their proposals create. The problems raised by a conscious direction of economic affairs on a national scale inevitably assume even greater dimensions when the same is attempted internationally. The conflict between planning and freedom cannot but become more serious as the similarity of standards and values among those submitted to a unitary plan diminishes. There need be little difficulty in planning the economic life of a family, comparatively little in a small community. But as the scale increases, the amount of agreement on the order of ends decreases and the necessity to rely on force and compulsion grows. In a small community common views on the relative importance of the main tasks, agreed standards of value, will exist on a great many subjects. But their number will

[1] On all these and on the following points, which can be touched upon only very briefly, see Professor Lionel Robbins's *Economic Planning and International Order*, 1937, *passim*.
[2] See particularly the significant book by James Burnham, *The Managerial Revolution*, 1941.

become less and less the wider we throw the net : and as there
is less community of views, the necessity to rely on force and
coercion increases.

The people of any one country may easily be persuaded to
make a sacrifice in order to assist what they regard as " their "
iron industry or " their " agriculture, or in order that in their
country nobody should sink below a certain level. So long as it
is a question of helping people whose habits of life and ways of
thinking are familiar to us, of correcting the distribution of
incomes among, or the working conditions of, people we can well
imagine and whose views on their appropriate status are fundamentally similar to ours, we are usually ready to make some
sacrifices. But one has only to visualise the problems raised by
economic planning of even an area such as Western Europe to
see that the moral bases for such an undertaking are completely
lacking. Who imagines that there exist any common ideals of
distributive justice such as will make the Norwegian fisherman
consent to forgo the prospect of economic improvement in order
to help his Portuguese fellow, or the Dutch worker to pay more
for his bicycle to help the Coventry mechanic, or the French
peasant to pay more taxes to assist the industrialisation of Italy ?

If most people are not willing to see the difficulty this is mainly
because, consciously or unconsciously, they assume that it will
be they who will settle these questions for the others, and because
they are convinced of their own capacity to do this justly and
equitably. English people, perhaps even more than others, begin
to realise what such schemes mean only when it is presented to
them that they might be a minority in the planning authority,
and that the main lines of the future economic development of
Great Britain might be determined by a non-British majority.
How many people in this country would be prepared to submit
to the decision of an international authority, however democratically constituted, which had power to decree that the development of the Spanish iron industry must have precedence over
similar development in South Wales, that the optical industry
had better be concentrated in Germany to the exclusion of Great
Britain, or that only fully refined petrol should be imported to
Great Britain and all the industries connected with refining
reserved for the producer countries ?

To imagine that the economic life of a vast area comprising
many different people can be directed or planned by democratic
procedure betrays a complete lack of awareness of the problems
such planning would raise. Planning on an international scale,
even more than is true on a national scale, cannot be anything
but a naked rule of force, an imposition by a small group on all
the rest of that sort of standard and employment which the

planners think suitable for the rest. If anything is certain it is
that *Grossraumwirtschaft* of the kind at which the Germans have
been aiming can be successfully realised only by a master race,
a *Herrenvolk*, ruthlessly imposing its aims and ideas on the rest.
It is a mistake to regard the brutality and the disregard of all the
wishes and ideals of the smaller people shown by the Germans
simply as a sign of their special wickedness ; it is the nature of
the task they have assumed which makes these things inevitable.
To undertake the direction of the economic life of people with
widely divergent ideals and values is to assume responsibilities
which commit one to the use of force ; it is to assume a position
where the best intentions cannot prevent one from being forced
to act in a way which to some of those affected must appear
highly immoral.[1]

This is true even if we assume the dominant power to be as
idealistic and unselfish as we can possibly conceive. But how
small is the likelihood that it will be unselfish, and how great are
the temptations ! I believe the standards of decency and fairness,
particularly with regard to international affairs, to be as high, if
not higher, in this than in any other country. Yet even now we
can hear people arguing that victory must be used to create conditions in which British industry will be able to utilise to the full
the particular equipment which it has built up during the war,
that the reconstruction of Europe must be so directed as to fit in
with the special requirements of the industries of this country,
and to secure to everybody in this country the kind of employment
for which he thinks himself most fit. The alarming thing about
these suggestions is not that they are made, but that they are made
in all innocence and regarded as a matter of course by decent
people who are completely unaware of the moral enormity which
the use of force for such purposes involves.[2]

* * * * *

[1] The experience in the colonial sphere, of this country as much as of any
other, has amply shown that even the mild forms of planning which we know
as colonial development involve, whether we wish it or not, the imposition of
certain values and ideals on those whom we try to assist. It is, indeed, this
experience which has made even the most internationally minded of colonial
experts so very sceptical of the practicability of an " international " administration of colonies.

[2] If anyone should still fail to see the difficulties, or cherish the belief that
with a little good will they can all be overcome, it will help if he tries to follow
the implications of central direction of economic activity applied on a world
scale. Can there be much doubt that this would mean a more or less conscious
endeavour to secure the dominance of the white man, and would rightly
be so regarded by all other races ? Till I find a sane person who seriously
believes that the European races will voluntarily submit to their standard of
life and rate of progress being determined by a World Parliament, I cannot
regard such plans as anything but absurd. But this does unfortunately not
preclude that particular measures, which could be justified only if the principle
of world direction were a feasible ideal, are seriously advocated.

Perhaps the most powerful agent in creating the belief in the possibility of a single central direction by democratic means of the economic life of many different peoples is the fatal delusion that if the decisions were left to the " people ", the community of interest of the working classes would readily overcome the differences which exist between the ruling classes. There is every reason to expect that with world planning the clash of economic interests which arises now about the economic policy of any one nation would in fact appear in even fiercer form as a clash of interests between whole peoples which could be decided only by force. On the questions which an international planning authority would have to decide, the interests and opinions of the working classes of the different people will inevitably be as much in conflict, and there will be even less of a commonly accepted basis for an equitable settlement, than there is with respect to different classes in any one country. To the worker in a poor country the demand of his more fortunate colleague to be protected against his low wage competition by minimum wage legislation, supposedly in his interest, is frequently no more than a means to deprive him of his only chance to better his conditions by overcoming natural disadvantages by working at wages lower than his fellows in other countries. And to him the fact that he has to give the product of ten hours of his labour for the product of five hours of the man elsewhere who is better equipped with machinery is as much " exploitation " as that practised by any capitalist.

It is fairly certain that in a planned international system the wealthier and therefore most powerful nations would to a very much greater degree than in a free economy become the object of hatred and envy of the poorer ones : and the latter, rightly or wrongly, would all be convinced that their position could be improved much more quickly if they were only free to do what they wished. Indeed, if it comes to be regarded as the duty of the international authority to bring about distributive justice between the different peoples, it is no more than a consistent and inevitable development of socialist doctrine that class strife would become a struggle between the working classes of the different countries.

There is at present a great deal of muddle-headed talk about " planning to equalise standards of life ". It is instructive to consider in a little more detail one of these proposals to see what precisely it involves. The area for which at the present moment our planners are particularly fond of drawing up such schemes is the Danube Basin and South-Eastern Europe. There can be no doubt· about the urgent need for amelioration of economic conditions in this region, from humanitarian and economic considerations as well as in the interest of the future peace of Europe, nor that this can be achieved only in a political setting different from that of the past. But this is not the same thing as to wish to see economic life in this region to be directed according to a single master plan, to foster the development of the different industries according to a schedule laid down beforehand in a way which makes the success of local initiative dependent on being approved by the central authority and being incorporated in its plan. One cannot, for example, create a kind of " Tennessee Valley Authority " for the Danube Basin without thereby determining beforehand for many years to come the relative rate of progress of the different races inhabiting this area, or without subordinating all their individual aspirations and wishes to this task.

Planning of this kind must of necessity begin by fixing an order of priorities of the different claims. To plan for the deliberate equalisation of standards of living means that the different claims must be ranked according to merit, that some must be given precedence over others, and that the latter must wait their turn—even though those whose interests are thus relegated may be convinced, not only of their better right, but also of their ability to reach their goal sooner if they were only given freedom to act on their own devices. There exists no basis which allows us to decide whether the claims of the poor Rumanian peasant are more or less urgent than those of the still poorer Albanian, or the needs of the Slovakian mountain shepherd greater than those of his Slovenian colleague. But if the raising of their standards of life is to be effected according to a unitary plan, somebody must deliberately balance the merits of all these claims and decide between them. And once such a plan is put into execution, all the resources of the planned area must serve that plan—there can be no exemption for those who feel they could do better for themselves. Once their claim has been given a lower rank, they will have to work for the prior satisfaction of the needs of those who have been given preference. In such a state of affairs *everybody* will rightly feel that he is worse off than he might be if some other plan had been adopted, and that it is the decision and the might of the dominant powers which have condemned him to a place less favourable than he thinks is due to him. To attempt such a thing in a region peopled by small nations, each of which believes equally fervently in its own superiority over the others, is to undertake a task which can be performed only by the use of force. What it would amount to in practice is that British decisions and British power would have to settle whether the standards of the Macedonian or the Bulgarian peasant should be raised faster, whether the Czech or the Hungarian miner should more rapidly approach Western standards. It does not need much knowledge of human nature, and certainly only a little knowledge of the people of Central Europe, to see that whatever the decision imposed, there will be many, probably a majority, to whom the particular order chosen will appear supreme injustice, and that their common hatred will soon turn against the power which, however disinterestedly, in fact decides their fate.

Though there are no doubt many people who honestly believe that if they were allowed to handle the job they would be able to settle all these problems justly and impartially, and who would be genuinely surprised to find suspicion and hatred turning against them, they would probably be the first to apply force when those whom they mean to benefit prove recalcitrant, and to show themselves quite ruthless in coercing people in what is presumed to be their own interests. What these dangerous idealists do not see is that where the assumption of a moral responsibility involves that one's moral views should by force be made to prevail over those dominant in other communities, the assumption of such responsibility may place one in a position in which it becomes impossible to act morally. To impose such an impossible moral task on the victorious nations is a certain way morally to corrupt and discredit them.

By all means let us assist the poorer people as much as we can in their own efforts to build up their lives and to raise their standards of living. An international authority can be very just and contribute enormously to economic prosperity if it merely keeps order and creates conditions in which the people can develop their own life; but it is impossible to be just or to let people live their own life if the central authority doles out raw materials and allocates markets, if every spontaneous effort has to be " approved " and nothing can be done without the sanction of the central authority.

* * * * *

After the discussions in earlier chapters it is hardly necessary to stress that these difficulties cannot be met by conferring on the various international authorities " merely " specific economic powers. The belief that this is a practical solution rests on the fallacy that economic planning is merely a technical task, which can be solved in a strictly objective manner by experts, and that the really vital things would still be left in the hands of the political authorities. Any international economic authority, not subject to a superior political power, even if strictly confined to a particular field, could easily exercise the most tyrannical and irresponsible power imaginable. Exclusive control of an essential commodity or service (as, for example, air transport) is in effect one of the most far-reaching powers which can be conferred on any authority. And as there is scarcely anything which could not be justified by " technical necessities " which no outsider could effectively question—or even by humanitarian and possibly entirely sincere arguments about the needs of some specially ill-favoured group which could not be helped in any other way—there is little possibility of controlling that power. The kind of organisation of the resources of the world under more or less autonomous bodies, which now so often finds favour in the most surprising quarters, a system of comprehensive monopolies recognised by all of the national governments, but subject to none, would inevitably become the worst of all conceivable rackets—even if those entrusted with their administration should prove the most faithful guardians of the particular interests placed in their care.

One need only seriously consider the full implications of such apparently innocuous proposals, widely regarded as the essential basis of the future economic order, such as the conscious control and distribution of the supply of essential raw materials, in order to see what appalling political difficulties and moral dangers they create. The controller of the supply of any such raw material as petrol or timber, rubber or tin, would be the master of the fate of whole industries and countries. In deciding whether to allow the supply to increase and the price or the income of the producers to fall, he would decide whether some country is to be allowed to start some new industry or whether it is to be precluded from doing so. While he " protects " the standards of life of those he regards as specially entrusted to his care, he will deprive many who are in a much worse position of their best and perhaps only chance to improve it. If all essential raw materials were thus controlled there would indeed be no new industry, no new venture on which the people of a country could embark without the permission of the controllers, no plan for development or improvement which could not be frustrated by their veto. The same is true of international arrangement for " sharing " of markets and even more so of the control of investment and the development of natural resources.

It is curious to observe how those who pose as the most hard-boiled realists, and who lose no opportunity of casting ridicule on the " utopianism " of those who believe in the possibility of an international political order, yet regard as more practicable the much more intimate and irresponsible interference with the lives of the different peoples which economic planning involves ; and believe that, once hitherto undreamed-of power is given to an international government, which has just been represented as not even capable of enforcing a simple Rule of Law, this greater power will be used in so unselfish and so obviously just a manner as to command general consent.   If anything is evident it should be that, while nations might abide by formal rules on which they have agreed, they will never submit to the direction which international economic planning involves—that while they may agree on the rules of the game, they will never agree on the order of preference in which the rank of their own needs and the rate at which they are allowed to advance is fixed by majority vote.   Even if, at first, the peoples should, under some illusion about the meaning of such pro-posals, agree to transfer such powers to an international authority, they would soon find out that what they have delegated is not merely a technical task, but the most comprehensive power over their very lives.

What is evidently at the back of the minds of the not altogether unpracticable " realists " who advocate these schemes is that, while the great Powers will be unwilling to submit to any superior authority, they will be able to use those " international " authori-ties to impose their will on the smaller nations within the area in which they exercise hegemony.   There is so much " realism " in this that by thus camouflaging the planning authorities as " international " it might be easier to achieve the condition under which international planning is alone practicable, namely, that it is in effect done by one single predominant power.   This disguise would, however, not alter the fact that for all the smaller states it would mean a much more complete subjection to an external power, to which no real resistance would any longer be possible, than would be involved in the renunciation of a clearly defined part of political sovereignty.

It is significant that the most passionate advocates of a centrally directed economic New Order for Europe should display, like their Fabian and German prototypes, the most complete disregard of the individuality and of the rights of small nations.   The views of Professor Carr, who in this sphere even more than in that of internal policy is representative of the trend towards totalitarianism in this country, have already made one of his professional colleagues ask the very pertinent question : " If the Nazi way with small sovereign states is indeed to become the common form, what is the war about ? " [1]   Those who have observed how much disquiet and alarm some recent utterances on these questions in papers as different as *The Times* and the *New Statesmen* [2] have caused among our smaller Allies will have

[1] Professor C. A. W. Manning, in a review of Professor Carr's *Conditions of Peace* in the International Affairs Review Supplement, June 1942.
[2] It is significant in more than one respect that, as was recently observed in one of the weekly journals, " one had already begun to expect a touch of the Carr flavour in the *New Statesman* pages as well as in those of *The Times* (" Four Winds " in *Time and Tide*, February 20, 1943).

little doubt how much this attitude is even now resented among
our closest friends, and how easy it will be to dissipate the stock
of goodwill which has been laid up during the war if these
advisers are followed.

* * * * *

Those who are so ready to ride roughshod over the rights of
small states are, of course, right in one thing : we cannot hope
for order or lasting peace after this war if states, large or small,
regain unfettered sovereignty in the economic sphere. But this
does not mean that a new super-state must be given powers which
we have not learnt to use intelligently even on a national scale,
that an international authority ought to be given power to direct
individual nations how to use their resources. It means merely
that there must be a power which can restrain the different
nations from action harmful to their neighbours, a set of rules
which defines what a state may do, and an authority capable of
enforcing these rules. The powers which such an authority
would need are mainly of a negative kind : it must above all be
able to say " no " to all sorts of restrictive measures.

Far from its being true that, as is now widely believed, we
need an international economic authority while the states can at
the same time retain their unrestricted political sovereignty,
almost exactly the opposite is true. What we need and can hope
to achieve is not more power in the hands of irresponsible international economic authorities, but, on the contrary, a superior
political power which can hold the economic interests in check,
and in the conflict between them can truly hold the scales, because
it is itself not mixed up in the economic game. The need is for
an international political authority which, without power to direct
the different people what they must do, must be able to restrain
them from action which will damage others. The powers which
must devolve on an international authority are not the new
powers assumed by the states in recent times, but that minimum
of powers without which it is impossible to preserve peaceful
relationships, i.e. essentially the powers of the ultra-liberal
" *laissez-faire* " state. And even more than in the national
sphere, it is essential that these powers of the international
authority should be strictly circumscribed by the Rule of Law.
The need for such a super-national authority becomes indeed
greater as the individual states more and more become units
of economic administration, the actors rather than merely the
supervisors of the economic scene, and as therefore any friction
is likely to arise not between individuals but between states as
such.

The form of international government under which certain

strictly defined powers are transferred to an international authority, while in all other respects the individual countries remain
responsible for their internal affairs, is, of course, that of federation. We must not allow the numerous ill-considered and often
extremely silly claims made on behalf of a federal organisation
of the whole world during the height of the propaganda for
" Federal Union " to obscure the fact that the principle of
federation is the only form of association of different peoples
which will create an international order without putting an undue
strain on their legitimate desire for independence.[1] Federalism
is, of course, nothing but the application to international affairs
of democracy, the only method of peaceful change man has
yet invented. But it is a democracy with definitely limited
powers. Apart from the more impracticable ideal of fusing
different countries into a single centralised state (the desirability
of which is far from obvious) it is the only way in which the
ideal of international law can be made a reality. We must not
deceive ourselves that in calling in the past the rules of international behaviour international law we were doing more than
expressing a pious wish. When we want to prevent people from
killing each other we are not content to issue a declaration that
killing is undesirable, but we give an authority power to prevent
it. In the same way there can be no international law without
a power to enforce it. The obstacle to the creation of such an
international power was very largely the idea that it need command
all the practically unlimited powers which the modern state
possesses. But with the division of power under the federal
system this is by no means necessary.

This division of power would inevitably act at the same time
also as a limitation of the power of the whole as well as of the
individual state. Indeed many of the kinds of planning which
are now fashionable would probably become altogether impossible.[2] But it would by no means constitute an obstacle to
all planning. It is, in fact, one of the main advantages of federation that it can be so devised as to make most of the harmful
planning difficult while leaving the way free for all desirable
planning. It prevents, or can be made to prevent, most forms
of restrictionism. And it confines international planning to the
fields where true agreement can be reached—not only between the

---

[1] It is a great pity that the flood of federalist publications which in recent
years has descended upon us has deprived the few important and thoughtful
works among them of the attention they deserved. One which in particular
ought to be carefully consulted when the time comes for the framing of a new
political structure of Europe is Dr. W. Ivor Jennings's small book on *A Federation for Western Europe* (1940).
[2] See on this the author's article on " Economic Conditions of Inter-State
Federation ", *The New Commonwealth Quarterly*, vol. V, September 1939.

" interests " immediately concerned, but among all those affected. The desirable forms of planning which can be effected locally and without the need of restrictive measures, are left free and in the hands of those best qualified to undertake it. It is even to be hoped that within a federation, where there will no longer exist the same reasons for making the individual states as strong as possible, the process of centralisation of the past may in some measure be reversed and some devolution of powers from the state to the local authorities become possible.

It is worth recalling that the idea of the world at last finding peace through the absorption of the separate states in large federated groups and ultimately perhaps in one single federation, far from being new, was indeed the ideal of almost all the liberal thinkers of the nineteenth century. From Tennyson, whose much quoted vision of the " battle of the air " is followed by a vision of the federation of the people which will follow their last great fight, right down to the end of the century the final achievement of a federal organisation remained the ever-recurring hope of a next great step in the advance of civilisation. Nine-teenth-century liberals may not have been fully aware *how* essential a complement of their principles a federal organisation of the different states formed [1]; but there were few among them who did not express their belief in it as an ultimate goal.[2]   It was only with the approach of our twentieth century that before the triumphant rise of *Realpolitik* these hopes came to be regarded as unpracticable and utopian.

* * * * *

We shall not rebuild civilisation on the large scale. It is no accident that on the whole there was more beauty and decency to be found in the life of the small peoples, and that among the large ones there was more happiness and content in proportion as they had avoided the deadly blight of centralisation. Least of all shall we preserve democracy or foster its growth if all the power and most of the important decisions rest with an organisation far too big for the common man to survey or comprehend. Nowhere has democracy ever worked well without a great measure of local self-government, providing a school of political training for the people at large as much as for their future leaders.

[1] See on this Professor Robbins's already quoted book, pp. 240–57.
[2] As late as the closing years of the nineteenth century Henry Sidgwick thought it " not beyond the limits of a sober forecast to conjecture that some future integration may take place in the West European states : and if it should take place, it seems probable that the example of America will be followed, and that the new political aggregate will be formed on the basis of a federal polity " (*The Development of European Polity*, published posthumously in 1903, p. 439).

It is only where responsibility can be learnt and practised in affairs with which most people are familiar, where it is the awareness of one's neighbour rather than some theoretical knowledge of the needs of other people which guides action, that the ordinary man can take a real part in public affairs because they concern the world he knows. Where the scope of the political measures becomes so large that the necessary knowledge is almost exclusively possessed by the bureaucracy, the creative impulses of the private person must flag. I believe that here the experience of the small countries like Holland and Switzerland contains much from which even the most fortunate larger countries like Great Britain can learn. We shall all be the gainers if we can create a world fit for small states to live in.

But the small can preserve their independence in the international as in the national sphere only within a true system of law which guarantees both that certain rules are invariably enforced and that the authority which has the power to enforce these cannot use it for any other purpose. While for its task of enforcing the common law the super-national authority must be very powerful, its constitution must at the same time be so designed that it prevents the international as well as the national authorities from becoming tyrannical. We shall never prevent the abuse of power if we are not prepared to limit power in a way which occasionally may also prevent its use for desirable purposes. The great opportunity we shall have at the end of this war is that the great victorious powers, by themselves first submitting to a system of rules which they have the power to enforce, may at the same time acquire the moral right to impose the same rules upon others.

An international authority which effectively limits the powers of the state over the individual will be one of the best safeguards of peace. The international Rule of Law must become a safeguard as much against the tyranny of the state over the individual as against the tyranny of the new super-state over the national communities. Neither an omnipotent super-state, nor a loose association of " free nations ", but a community of nations of free men must be our goal. We have long pleaded that it had become impossible to behave in international affairs as we thought it desirable because others would not play the game. The coming settlement will be the opportunity to show that we have been sincere and that we are prepared to accept the same restrictions on our freedom of action which in the common interest we think it necessary to impose upon others.

Wisely used, the federal principle of organisation may indeed prove the best solution of some of the world's most difficult problems. But its application is a task of extreme difficulty and we are not likely to succeed if in an over-ambitious attempt we strain it beyond its capacity. There will probably exist a strong tendency to make any new international organisation all-comprehensive and world-wide; and there will, of course, be an imperative need for some such comprehensive organisation, some new League of Nations. The great danger is that, if in the attempt to rely exclusively on this world organisation it is charged with all the tasks which it seems desirable to place in the hands of an international organisation, they will not in fact be adequately performed. It has always been my conviction that such ambitions were at the root of the weakness of the League of Nations : that in the (unsuccessful) attempt to make it world-wide it had to be made weak, and that a smaller and at the same time more powerful League might have been a better instrument to preserve peace. I believe that these considerations still hold and that a degree of co-operation could be achieved between, say, the British Empire and the nations of Western Europe and probably the United States which would not be possible on a world scale. The comparatively close association which a Federal Union represents will not at first be practicable beyond perhaps even as narrow a region as part of Western Europe, though it may be possible gradually to extend it.

It is true that with the formation of such regional federations the possibility of war between the different blocs still remains, and that to reduce this risk as much as possible we must rely on a larger and looser association. My point is that the need for some such other organisation should not form an obstacle to a closer association of those countries which are more similar in their civilisation, outlook, and standards. While we must aim at preventing future wars as much as possible, we must not believe that we can at one stroke create a permanent organisation which will make all war in any part of the world entirely impossible. We should not only not succeed in such an attempt, but we should thereby probably spoil our chances of achieving success in a more limited sphere. As is true with respect to other great evils, the measures by which war might be made altogether impossible for the future may well be worse than even war itself. If we can reduce the risk of friction likely to lead to war, this is probably all we can reasonably hope to achieve.

CONCLUSION

THE purpose of this book has not been to sketch a detailed programme of a desirable future order of society. If with regard to international affairs we have gone a little beyond its essentially critical task, it was because in this field we may soon be called upon to create a framework within which future growth may have to proceed for a long time to come. A great deal will depend on how we use the opportunity we shall then have. But whatever we do, it can only be the beginning of a new, long, and arduous process in which we all hope we shall gradually create a world very different from that which we knew during the last quarter of a century. It is at least doubtful whether at this stage a detailed blueprint of a desirable internal order of society would be of much use—or whether anyone is competent to furnish it. The important thing now is that we shall come to agree on certain principles and free ourselves from some of the errors which have governed us in the recent past. However distasteful such an admission may be, we must recognise that we had before this war once again reached a stage where it is more important to clear away the obstacles with which human folly has encumbered our path and to release the creative energy of individuals than to devise further machinery for " guiding " and " directing " them— to create conditions favourable to progress rather than to " plan progress ". The first need is to free ourselves of that worst form of contemporary obscurantism which tries to persuade us that what we have done in the recent past was all either wise or inevitable. We shall not grow wiser before we learn that much that we have done was very foolish.

If we are to build a better world we must have the courage to make a new start—even if that means some *reculer pour mieux sauter*. It is not those who believe in inevitable tendencies who show this courage, not those who preach a " New Order " which is no more than a projection of the tendencies of the last forty years, and who can think of nothing better than to imitate Hitler. It is indeed those who cry loudest for the New Order who are most completely under the sway of the ideas which have created this war and most of the evils from which we suffer. The young are right if they have little confidence in the ideas which rule most of their elders. But they are mistaken or misled when they believe that these are still the liberal ideas of the nineteenth century, which in fact the younger generation hardly knows. Though we neither can wish, nor possess the power, to go back to the reality of the nineteenth century, we have the opportunity to realise its ideals—and they were not mean. We have little right to feel in this respect superior to our grandfathers; and we should never forget that it is we, the twentieth century, and not they, who have made a mess of things. If they had not yet fully learnt what was necessary to create the world they wanted, the experience we have since gained ought to have equipped us better for the task. If in the first attempt to create a world of free men we have failed, we must try again. The guiding principle, that a policy of freedom for the individual is the only truly progressive policy, remains as true to-day as it was in the nineteenth century.

BIBLIOGRAPHICAL NOTE

The exposition of a point of view which for many years has been decidedly out of favour suffers from the difficulty that, within the compass of a few chapters, it is not possible to discuss more than some aspects of it. For the reader whose outlook has been formed entirely by the views that have been dominant during the last twenty years this will scarcely be sufficient to provide the common ground required for profitable discussion. But although unfashionable, the views of the author of the present book are not so singular as they may appear to some readers. His basic outlook is the same as that of a steadily growing number of writers in many countries whose studies have led them independently to similar conclusions. The reader who would like to acquaint himself further with what he may have found an unfamiliar but not uncongenial climate of opinion, may find useful the following list of some of the more important works of this kind, including several in which the essentially critical character of the present essay is supplemented by a fuller discussion of the structure of a desirable future society.

W. H. CHAMBERLIN. *A False Utopia. Collectivism in Theory and Practice.* (Duckworth) 1937.

F. D. GRAHAM. *Social Goals and Economic Institutions.* (Princeton University Press) 1942.

E. HALÉVY. *L'Ere des Tyrannies.* Paris (Gallimard) 1938. English versions of two of the most important essays in this volume will be found in *Economica*, February 1941, and in *International Affairs*, 1934.

G. HALM, L. v. MISES, and others. *Collectivist Economic Planning,* ed. by F. A. Hayek. (Routledge) 1937.

W. H. HUTT. *Economists and the Public.* (Cape) 1935.

W. LIPPMANN, *An Inquiry into the Principles of the Good Society.* (Allen & Unwin) 1937.

L. v. MISES. *Socialism,* trsl. by J. Kahane. (Cape) 1936.

R. MUIR. *Liberty and Civilisation.* (Cape) 1940.

M. POLANYI. *The Contempt of Freedom.* (Watts) 1940.

W. RAPPARD. *The Crisis of Democracy.* (University of Chicago Press) 1938.

L. C. ROBBINS. *Economic Planning and International Order.* (Macmillan) 1937.

L. C. ROBBINS. *The Economic Basis of Class Conflict and Other Essays in Political Economy.* (Macmillan) 1939.

L. C. ROBBINS. *The Economic Causes of War.* (Cape) 1939.

W. ROEPKE. *Die Gesellschaftskrisis der Gegenwart.* Zürich (Eugen Rentsch) 1942.

L. ROUGIER. *Les mystiques économiques.* Paris (Librairie Medicis) 1938.

F. A. VOIGT. *Unto Caesar.* (Constable) 1938.

The following of the "Public Policy Pamphlets" edited by the University of Chicago Press—

H. SIMONS. *A Positive Program for Laissez-Faire. Some Proposals for a Liberal Economic Policy.* 1934.

H. D. GIDEONSE. *Organised Scarcity and Public Policy.* 1939.

F. A. HERMENS. *Democracy and Proportional Representation.* 1940.

W. SULZBACH. *" Capitalist Warmongers " : A Modern Superstition.*
1942.
M. A. HEILPERIN. *Economic Policy and Democracy.* 1943.

There are also important German and Italian works of a similar character which, in consideration for their authors, it would be unwise at present to mention by name.

To this list I add the titles of three books which more than any others known to me help one to understand the system of ideas ruling our enemies and the differences which separate their minds from ours,

E. B. ASHTON. *The Fascist, His State and Mind.* (Putnam) 1937.
F. W. FOERSTER. *Europe and the German Question.* (Sheed) 1940.
H. KANTOROWICZ. *The Spirit of English Policy and the Myth of the Encirclement of Germany.* (Allen & Unwin) 1931.

and that of a remarkable recent work on the modern history of Germany which is not as well known in this country as it deserves :

F. SCHNABEL. *Deutsche Geschichte im* 19. *Jahrhundert.* 4 vols.
Freiburg, i. B. 1929–37.

Perhaps the best guides through some of our contemporary problems will still be found in the works of some of the great political philosophers of the liberal age, a de Tocqueville or Lord Acton, and, to go even farther back, Benjamin Constant, Edmund Burke, and the Federalist papers of Madison, Hamilton, and Jay, generations to whom liberty was still a problem and a value to be defended, where ours at the same time takes it for granted and neither realises whence the danger threatens nor has the courage to emancipate itself from the doctrines which endanger it.

INDEX